SEASONED SPIRITUALITY

a compendium of characterizations imparting charisms to live by

To Edna—,
Read & discover new charisms
of your own!
Jean Riise Leffler

By Jean Riise Leffler

Also by Jean Riise Leffler

Spirituality at Sunrise

Author's Note: The Biblical quotes throughout are from the New
Revised Standard Version

Seasoned Spirituality

Published on Demand by CreateSpace.com, Charleston, SC

Cover and Interior Designs, and Line Drawings by Jean Riise Leffler

ISBN: 9781495988134

Also by Jean Riise Leffler

Spirituality at Sunrise

DEDICATION

To Grandma and her three sisters, who were born to German immigrants at the turn of the last century, I dedicate this book. Each sister, my great-aunts, influenced my life in a positive way. Aunt Tessie served as an example of dedicated prayerful living; Aunt Clara was an example for me by rolling up her sleeves and going to work after the tragic suicide death of Uncle Charlie - but she didn't forget to laugh along the way; Aunt Anna taught me that being beautiful comes in all sizes. As a grandma and great aunts, they instilled in me a fearless appreciation for my elders and their personal stories. Because of their spiritual legacies, their charisms, I am a better person and I welcome my own aging process.

"Tell the older women to be reverent in behavior, not to be slanderers or slaves to drink; they are to teach what is good, so that they may encourage the young women to love their husbands, to love their children, to be self controlled, chaste, good managers of the household, kind, being submissive to their husbands so that the word of God may not be discredited."

Titus 2:3-5

INTRODUCTION

Gardening involves such basic tasks as cultivating the soil, planting seeds, feeding and caring for tender plants, and harvesting the fruits of one's labor. Choosing a career in the field of caring for the aged was not dissimilar from gardening for me. I spent most of twenty years cultivating a life of learning from the elderly. Working in senior center settings afforded me the privilege of planting seeds of friendship with some very interesting folks and working shoulder to shoulder with active senior volunteers. While working in assisted living and long term care homes I learned the importance of caring for those hiding beneath hard-shelled exteriors. It was in that setting that I was eventually able to uncover tender interiors hidden away. The harvest was often the hardest aspect of working with the elderly. True, it troubled me to say good-bye to good people but in time I came to appreciate that each one left me a legacy, a charism, not of monetary value but spiritual value. Even now, as I relate these characterizations, I shed a few tears – not of sorrow but of gratitude. My senior friends taught me how to age, and do it well. Their lives exemplified courage and resolve despite aches and pains, tragedy and sadness. They found the good in the bad as they followed St. Paul's instruction to the Thessalonians, "give thanks in all circumstances; for this is the will of God in Christ Jesus for you." (1 Thessalonians 5:18) They imparted a value system that would have taken me a lifetime to develop on my own, without their life-examples.

I invite you to stand at the edge of life's garden. The gate is tired though still functional and allows entry to a very special place. Look past the rickety gate. At a distance a giant mature tree stands tall at the center of the garden. Think of the Garden of Eden as described in the book of Genesis: "Out of the ground the Lord God made to grow every tree that is pleasant to the sight and good for food, the tree of life also in the midst of the garden, and the tree of knowledge of good and evil." (Genesis 2: 9)

The Central Tree in the center of life's garden appears to be at its full growth; however, that is an illusion. As long as a tree lives it marks the seasons: spring with new growth; summer with blooms; autumn with golden colors; and winter with snow-laden beauty. At each season, the

Central Tree continues to grow and change while contributing to the environment until its death. Sometimes there is contribution even beyond death.

Similarly humans also contribute to the environment – to society – until death, and often beyond. Compare the life of our Central Tree to the life of the aged. Notice the obvious. Neither the tree nor the Senior Adult gets to the 'mature stage' by being inflexible. Our tree displays strength; the elder also displays strength through character, courage and charism (spiritual purpose). Both must yield enough to bend with the prevailing breezes and fierce storms. The Central Tree demonstrates the soul of the earth; the Senior Adult demonstrates the soul of society's value system.

Trees, forests, and gardens must be treasured, preserved and cherished. Without care, their resulting decline puts our environment at risk. Similarly, the decline of the family ethic puts our society at risk. Our core values in life come from our roots – our American values, our family values, our faith values. Even without a personal family tree rooted in a good value system we can ensure we grow to be strong, straight individuals with good mores. Where and how can we nurture the value system needed to sustain a happy and healthy life? One need only observe, and emulate, the lives of good examples. Learn from the experiences of others.

The aged, like trees, are cherished in some cultures, disdained in others, but always needed for their legacies. My grandmother used to say, "old age is for the birds". She was right. Aging isn't easy but it must be embraced. Sure, there is pain, but there is also beauty, love, and most importantly time. As I age I have time to reminisce about my childhood, my trials and tribulations and my elders. While I was spending my career listening to others' stories I used to analyze their coping skills and I discerned what I am compelled to pass on to my family and to you. Within these pages are many of the good, solid, ethical values that our fractured families and broken society have no opportunity to teach. My own experiences provide me with my own life ideals but when I couple them with those of the wonderful 'old folks' that I have had the privilege of knowing I have so much more to share.

Seasoned Spirituality is a compendium of characterizations of some common people who taught me uncommon lessons about spiritual, familial, and physical life. Each elderly friend left me a valuable legacy. I call each legacy a CHARISM or a *spiritual purpose*.

The word *charism* is derived from the Greek word, 'charismata,' meaning gifts of grace. The biblical author, Paul uses the term *charism* to describe extraordinary, supernatural, and transitory gifts given freely for the spiritual welfare of the Christian community. Each legacy freely passed on to me by my elder models is a *charism* that could not be learned in a classroom, and each *charism* is worth far more than monetary or earthly treasure.

I met each character described within these pages at a time in his/her life when (s)he was considered obsolete. Observing their lives is like auditing the class of 'Life 101'. A smart person learns from their own experiences. A genius learns from the experiences of others! Appreciating their spiritual legacies, their *charisms*, is like accepting an honorary doctorate in spiritual purpose. Through these memoirs I hope to share with you *charisms* passed on to me by my senior friends.

"And the Lord God planted a garden in Eden...
Out of the ground the Lord God made to grow every tree that is pleasant to the sight and good for food,
The tree of life also in the midst of the garden..."
Genesis2:8-9

CHARACTERS

THE EARLIEST EXAMPLES
Ruth

Luther

Dorothy

SHELBYVILLE'S CITIZENS
Mary

Esther

Frances

Lillian

Florence

Mac and Lela

Lela and Mac

Lew and Pauline

Lorraine

Paul

Lourene

Anna

John and Peg

Lloyd

Ellen

LONG TERM CARE
Lura

Martha

Clyde

Henry and Dovie

Clara

Edna

SHORT BUT POWERFUL ANECDOTES
Luna

Harold

Kay

Tom *and* His Charism

THE ROOTS OF MY AWARENESS
Grandma

THE LAST WORDS

THE EARLIEST EXAMPLES

We pass along many legacies from past generations to future generations: heirloom furniture and jewelry. We bequest the family farm or the Victorian house to those who come after us. Legacies are often precious possessions and are handed down through our last will and testament. Legacies can be argued over, often pitting brother against brother, even with an iron-clad will in place. Those disagreements often result in the family treasure being divided or worse yet, sold.

The legacies described in these early character sketches are priceless spiritual treasures, charisms, with no monetary value. You cannot put a dollar amount on charisms of hospitality, courage, morality, faith, character, honesty, humor, or respect. These spiritual legacies were not free but they were shared freely – and in most cases – unknowingly, by well seasoned citizens. These life lessons depict a quality of being; a virtue; a shining spirit; a sensitivity to religious values. By adding the adjective 'spiritual' to the word 'legacy' you come to understand the true value of the gifts, the charisms, being passed on.

Throughout my life I've known many characters. Some were productive and others were useless, many were strong but some were weak, some were miserable but most were lighthearted. I learned something from every one of them, and I have never lost my passion for aging.

Here is something to contemplate: at what age is one considered elderly? Does the term describe a chronological age, or an attitudinal age? Is one old at 65? At 75? At 85? Over 90? One of my favorite 'oldsters'(80+ years old) that I have known used to describe 'old' as "twenty years older than I am right now." I think that is the most accurate description of elderly!

As I lead you through the rusty, rickety garden gate that reveals the Central Tree in our garden of **Seasoned Spirituality** our first stop is the Bible. We will visit it again throughout our tour. I invite you to stand at the base of the Central Tree; consider it as the Tree of Life that God intended to feed us physically and spiritually. Learn the great lessons of life, the charisms, left to us by the elderly described in these pages.

THE SPIRIT INTENDED

The book of Psalms is found in the center of the Old Testament of the Bible. There you find prayers of the heart. They were written to be sung in community. There are varying themes in the 150 psalms, from joy to lamentation; fear to trust; doubt to praise; and more. The psalms can bring a deep meaning to a devout prayer life as every word in the book of Psalms is a sacred word! The psalms follow the movement of human life from sin to conversion; from conversion to backsliding; from backsliding to sin; from sin to conversion; and again and again.

An appropriate psalm to use as the theme of Seasoned Spirituality is Psalm 90 because the psalmist writes of the cycle of life. This is a psalm that begins by expressing trust and recognition of God's steadfastness throughout history. It begins by confidently invoking God and grows in awareness of his mighty power.

> 1 "Lord, you have been our dwelling place
>   in all generations.
> 2 Before the mountains were brought forth,
>   or ever you had formed the earth and the
>   world, from everlasting to everlasting you are
>   God.
> 3 You turn us back to dust, and say, 'Turn back you
>   mortals!'
> 4 For a thousand years in your sight
>   are like yesterday when it is past,
>   or like a watch in the night.
> 5 You sweep them away; they are like a dream,
>   like grass that is renewed in the morning;
> 6 In the morning it flourishes and is renewed;
>   in the evening it fades and withers."

(Verses 1-6 NRSV)

RUTH

"But though I am an old (wo)man, I am but a young gardener."
Thomas Jefferson

My husband, children and I were 'strangers in a foreign land' living down a West Virginia 'holler' – a community nestled between two mountains. Many houses, including ours, were hand made of hand hewn lumber harvested from the land. We owned land on both sides of the road. Our log cabin sat on a hill and our log barn sat in the bottom land by a quiet creek. For the first months of our time there we were seen as outsiders. The rest of our time there we became honorary hill-billies!

Ruth was an active 70-something years old. She and her husband owned about 25 acres. Only one acre was flat, the rest was steep and wooded. Trees grew on the hillside, many were fruit trees: apple trees and pear trees mostly. The pear trees produced not just any pear, those pears were the biggest pears I had ever seen – or have seen since! I weighed one once, it was over ¾ pound! On their flat acre Ruth grew a prolific garden. Because Ruth's husband had lost a leg to diabetes, she worked the garden herself with an old work-horse of a tiller. What she grew, she canned, froze, or dried for the harsh Appalachian winter. Ruth was an expert cook and her apple pies were the first sold at church pie auctions. She canned the pears and made pear-sauce – like apple sauce but better.

Ruth taught me how to plant a garden, she encouraged my gardening skills though I was not always successful. I can still hear her chuckling because my home grown beets were the size of radishes! Despite my failures, she also taught me a lot about preserving the fruits of my labor. Those were home-making lessons that follow me to this day.

When the minister at Ruth's church was moved from the rural 'holler' to the big city, the little congregation needed a leader. In the days before women were commonly accepted in the pulpit, Ruth was urged to enter the sanctuary in a leadership role. Ruth was very knowledgeable about the Bible and had taught the adult women's Sunday school class for a long time with unpretentious self-confidence. Giving in to the coaxing, Ruth took on many responsibilities: of Sunday sermons, of directing the annual Christmas play and the week-long Vacation Bible School. She was tireless despite her advancing age.

Ruth had good, old fashioned values. She was hospitable, giving, spiritual, and loving. She passed each of those traits on to her family. Her many sons and daughters lived up and down the only paved road in the 'holler'. Ruth's grandchildren venerated her and Ruth's sun rose and set over them.

RUTH'S CHARISM

Our last winter in the hills and 'hollers' brought many hardships for my family: my husband lost his job and was forced to find work 600 miles away, leaving our daughters and me home to 'keep the light on'. While snow was still on the ground, something went wrong with our furnace. A workman from the gas company made a house call and gave me a troublesome diagnosis. A natural spring had leaked water into the gas line. Then he shut off the gas. As he got in his company truck he told me, 'call us when you get it fixed' and then he drove off! There we were: snow on the ground, two young children, no gas for cooking or heating, and my husband 600 miles away – I never felt so alone!

When Ruth heard of our plight she recruited her family to help us. One family member parked his RV in our driveway for the girls and I to be able to sleep in warmth. One son owned a backhoe. He drove it down the hollow into our large front yard and dug a ditch, to the gas company's specifications, for a new gas line. Another son rolled out the orange gas pipe provided by the gas company. Still another family member came and covered the ditch after the gas company folks inspected the work. Our new friend with the camper came on the weekend and helped my husband (on a brief visit home) hook up the gas service to the house. A small community came to share in the stress of the gas company's inspection of the new gas line. The reality of this story is that I never knew Ruth's kids and they didn't know me! They performed our rescue because of Ruth and the lessons, the charisms, she had taught them all their lives.

Ruth's spiritual legacy, her charism, went far beyond her children. Her example was a gift and taught me to help when a neighbor (or a stranger) is in trouble without waiting to be asked. Don't ask questions, just show up – especially if you own a backhoe!

"Ground that drinks up the rain falling on it repeatedly, and that produces a crop useful to those for whom it is cultivated, receives a blessing from God."

Hebrews 6:7

LUTHER

"The young man knows the rules, but the old man knows the exceptions."

Oliver Wendell Holmes

A 90-something year old widower drove a large maroon vintage Oldsmobile. He didn't let age or weather keep him housebound. Using his cane for security he ventured out in the rain or shine, snow or sleet. Luther lived alone and ate his main meal at lunch with his friends at the community center's Senior Meal Site on week days. He made soup or sandwiches to eat in front of the TV in the evenings. On the weekends his daughter came. She took him grocery shopping, played dominoes, and spent quality time with him. They were close but she lived in another town and worked full time through the week.

My husband was working in another state and only able to come home on weekends. While I was working at the dining site, Luther and I became 'week day' friends and I introduced my young daughters to him after school. This had been our third move across state lines we were becoming experts at 'collecting old friends'. My girls were hungry for a grandparent figure and Luther became a surrogate grandpa.

Often I picked my girls up after school and took them to visit Luther. He liked to bake and usually had homemade chocolate chip cookies to treat my daughters. Luther would entertain the girls by showing them his stereopticon and other antiques. They learned about the harsh life on the mid-western prairie at the turn of the last century. He listened intently to their tales of modern school days.

Luther would often bring homemade pies to me at the meal site when he came for lunch. Some of the other seniors began to tease him that I was his girlfriend. That embarrassed him and he was

15

afraid to dishonor me. He solved this dilemma by making make an early trip to the dining site before anyone else arrived to bring me a pie; then he would leave and return later at meal time. He brought me a chocolate cream pie one Christmas Eve before going to his daughter's for the holiday. While at her home, Luther died peacefully in his sleep.

LUTHER'S CHARISM

I am not too sure if Luther left me a legacy or I left him with a legacy. I may have provided him a 'weekday' friendship that filled his afternoons with company, but, more importantly, Luther provided me a friendship that included my daughters at a time we needed a sense of family.

I was not aware of our mutual spiritual connection until I met Luther's precious daughter at his funeral. Obviously my daughters and I had been the topic of many conversations during his weekend visits with her. She sought me out at the visitation to tell me "thank you, for befriending my father. Your visits were very important to him." I left the funeral home that evening in tears – tears of gratitude and loss. I was grateful for Luther. I was sad that I lost a friend. I was also grateful for the seed of awareness and respect for the aged that had been planted in my childhood by my grandmother and her sisters. I went home that evening and savored every bite of the last slice of Luther's chocolate cream pie. The charism? No kindness goes unnoticed.

"...everything is for your sake, so that grace, as it extends to more and more people, may increase thanksgiving, to the glory of God."

2 Corinthians 4:15

DOROTHY

*"Anyone who stops learning is old, whether twenty or eighty.
Anyone who keeps learning stays young."*

Henry Ford

After one of my moves across country, away from home and family I was especially lonely for my grandmother. Then I met Dorothy through church. There was an immediate connection and we developed a strong, long friendship despite a big age difference. Her husband, Jim, was disabled by heart disease and did not get out often. We lived nearby so I could and did walk to Dorothy's regularly to visit while my daughters were in school. Dorothy provided a port in my personal storm of loneliness.

While Jim was alive he and Dorothy put seed out to feed the birds every afternoon. Together, they could identify every kind of bird that came to their yard. They particularly liked to watch the doves because as Jim explained, "they symbolize God's peace." The house they shared for over 50 years was like a museum. Dorothy and Jim had not collected the antiques held within; they had used the items when they were new! She took good care of the tools of housekeeping, just as she took care of Jim through his long illness. But then, Dorothy took good care of everyone around her.

Dorothy was the quintessential country woman. Flowers and vegetables flourished in Dorothy's garden. Her garden was weed free and as neat as the proverbial pin. She and Jim were organic gardeners before anyone ever heard the term! They introduced me to companion planting – that technique matches the nutritional growing needs of plants and uses space sparingly. For instance, corn depletes the soil of nitrogen, beans restore the nitrogen to the soil and the corn stalks serve as trellises for the beans. Dorothy could grow anything! When she was 85, she planted a young cherry tree. She wrote me that she did not expect to see it bear fruit but was confident it would live on after she was gone. At 92, she was making jelly with the fruit from that tree!

Dorothy's hospitality was important to me when life planted me in her small community that consisted of a church, a post office, and a volunteer fire department. Dorothy's cooking skills were part of her hospitality plan. Her homemade soup was locally famous. It was known to cure colds, flu and homesickness. Her soup carried me through some lonely times.

Dorothy's round face beamed from behind the information desk at an area hospital for 13 years. Some called her an institution. The traditional pink jacket she wore reflected her warm smile. She greeted each hospital visitor as an old friend, handling complaints as gracefully as compliments. She comforted strangers in times of crisis and rejoiced with them when miracles occurred. Each Midwestern winter made it harder for Dorothy to negotiate the 20 miles of county roads and city streets to volunteer each week. The volunteer coordinator of the hospital would not hear of Dorothy's retiring when the commute became difficult for her to make on her own. Arrangements were made for family to drive Dorothy to and from her post each week. Finally, at the age of 87, Dorothy decided to pass the torch to someone younger, and she went home to rest.

Rest? Dorothy's idea of rest was certainly different than most. Her career at the hospital involved only one day a week. But she was busy every other day too. She served as president of her home economics club for years because the others claimed they were 'too old' to serve. She gave her time to the volunteer fire department auxiliary, served as a poll watcher at every election, cooked meals for the sick in the farming community, and so on. In between, she had doctor appointments of her own to monitor the effects of aging. If anyone ever needed a personal secretary, it was Dorothy.

At 87, while she was supposed to be resting, Dorothy found a new project. The local museum enlisted her help to provide a living history program at a nearby log cabin village. On Saturdays Dorothy shared stories of 'the old days' with visitors of all ages while demonstrating wood stove cooking – or quilting – or crocheting – or canning. She was a walking, talking history book.

Dorothy was a mainstay at her church far beyond her 'retirement'. She held church board positions, organized Vacation Bible School, cleaned the floors, led Bible studies, cooked funeral suppers, and even provided flowers for the altar from her own garden.

DOROTHY'S CHARISM

Dorothy lived to be 99 years and 10 months old. Her hearing declined in her later years, limiting her communication but not her spirit. She continued to write to me, especially at Valentine's Day in answer to my annual Christmas letter. The handwriting deteriorated over the years but her letters were always full of optimism, aspirations and especially happy family news. I fully believe that sharing God's love was her driving force. Dorothy never preached at, or to me but she was always a gentle example for me. Dorothy's bequest to me was to help me see that "I can do all things through Christ who strengthens me," (Philippians 4:13) and no matter how old I get I should not be reluctant to plant a tree because someone will benefit from its fruit!

"As the sun was setting, all those who had any who were sick with various diseases brought them to him; and he laid his hands on each of them and cured them."

Luke 4:40

19

SHELBYVILLE'S CITIZENS

Like many Midwestern towns, Shelbyville, Indiana, grew out from a central circle of businesses. Three-story 100-year-old buildings rim the busy hub. The stores are predominately owned and operated by mom-and-pop, locally owned and operated businesses. The town circle is not a place to find chain-stores. A large decorative water fountain supports a stone sculpture of a mountain-man holding two bear cubs high, as if in triumph. These are the Bears of Blue River. Flanking the fountain are two city-owned parking lots. A busy four-lane, State Road 9, runs north and south around this landmark fountain and parking lots. Washington Street, a busy city street, runs east and west at ¼ turn around the circle.

The latest numbers show that more than 13% of city residents are over 65 and that number surely increases every year. The local senior service agency provides needed services for that population, specializing in aiding the frail, typically over-80, elderly. Federal, state, and county funding help support the agency's budget, but that money must be supplemented by monies raised by the agency itself through corporate campaigns and special events.

Keeping the seniors up and moving was my job. In the position of center director I was tasked with developing a full range of activities and coordinating the fund raising events. In my years of service for the agency I met the most amazing people. Their faces were creased and wrinkled with age. Their fingers were gnarled by arthritis. Their eyes were clouded by cataracts. Beyond their prime? Maybe, but they were not out of the game. By their very being, these aged friends taught me life lessons that cannot be learned anywhere else but at their side. These were common people who taught uncommon lessons about life.

As we progress through life, we seldom know how we touch others. We seldom consider how our lives influence others. Our last will and testament passes on our material belongings. But how do we pass on our values and spirituality? I spent the better part of twenty-plus years working with, caring for, and learning from the elderly. These old friends (meant literally) left me far greater treasures than any "stuff" that they could have willed to me. My purpose in writing these characterizations is to give you a crash course in life and pass on the lessons, the charisms, I learned, not at their knee but at their shoulder – close to their heart and soul.

THE SPIRIT INTENDED CONTINUES

Psalm 90 goes on to describe the author's awareness, apprehension and trepidation that God is the ultimate magistrate in the final judgment. In this segment of Psalm 90, the author assures God that he recognizes the approaching end of life as noted in verses 9 and 10. The psalmist invokes God to teach us to behave well and develop wisdom.

> 7 "For we are consumed by your anger;
> by your wrath we are overwhelmed.
> 8 You have set out our iniquities before you,
> our secret sins in the light of your countenance.
> 9 For all our days pass away under your wrath;
> our years come to an end like a sigh.
> 10 The days of our life are seventy years,
> or perhaps eighty, if we are strong;
> even then their span is only toil and trouble;
> they are soon gone, and we fly away.
> 11 Who considers the power of your anger?
> Your wrath is as great as the fear that is due to you.
> 12 So teach us to count our days that we may gain
> a wise heart."
>
> (verses 7-12 NRSV)

MARY

*"So much has been said and sung of the beautiful young girls.
Why don't somebody wake up to the beauty of old women?"*
                                                    Harriet Beecher Stowe

Mary's story is an epic of life's hardships. She was three when her mother died. Jim, her brother was ten. Caleb, their father, was devastated by the death of his wife and overwhelmed by the task of raising a three-year-old little girl. Rural Indiana was on the fringes of 'civilization' at that time and there were not many jobs. Caleb found what work he could on farms, dairies and at sawmills.

Jim, big for his age, would work in the fields along-side of Caleb. Mary would sit at the ends of the rows and play with the doll her mother had made for her the Christmas before she died. In the evenings Caleb would grieve and drink himself to sleep. When morning came, the little family would move to the next farm and repeat the pattern.

Caleb knew this life was no way to raise a pretty little girl like Mary, yet he saw no way to provide a stable home. With his heart heavy he took Mary to an orphanage. Jim stayed with Caleb and they continued to move from job to job. Occasionally, when the father and son pair found work near the orphanage, they would visit Mary.

Life was bearable for Mary at the orphanage. She was clean, dry and safe. She attended classes and excelled at sewing, knitting and other 'girl skills'. On Sundays all the girls at the orphanage were dressed in their best ruffled dresses with hair bows adorning their curls. They were paraded in front of prospective parents. Couples who were anxious to adopt came to 'pick out a daughter.' Mary was never chosen. When she told me this story, she said she felt she was never pretty enough. So Mary lived out her childhood at the orphanage.

Upon leaving the orphanage, Mary chose to study and became a beautician. This profession would give her a livelihood and the security for which she had always hoped. There was a sadness though, despite her independence, she yearned for a family.

As a young woman, Mary met and married a fine man. He was good to her and they were happy for six years. Mary hoped for a daughter to love but was childless when he was killed in a tragic automobile accident. Mary was alone again. Accustomed to disappointment she did not allow this to destroy her.

Her reputation of giving good hair care led a handsome young accountant to Mary's shop. Robert and Mary became quite an item and were soon married. They spent several happy years together. Sadly, Mary was childless when he died of Cancer. Once again, Mary was alone. However she remained ever resilient.

Time was marching on and Mary came to accept the reality that she would never have children. She made the best of life. Her friends' children became very special to her.

While working in a major department store's beauty shop she met John. He was a traveling sales representative for a jewelry supplier. Mary and John dated and eventually married. This third marriage was not a happy one. John was demanding, pessimistic and possessive of Mary's time. In retirement, Mary enjoyed the activities at the senior center while John preferred to stay home – with Mary at his side.

When I first met Mary, she was wearing a colorful bow in her silver grey hair. She wore a permanent, genuine smile highlighting her face. She didn't need make-up, her inner beauty shone through the layers of her life's disappointments. Mary brought a breath of fresh air to the senior center every time she walked in the door. She always had warm and encouraging words for others. She visited the senior center only once a week. She would have loved to visit more often but wanted, desperately, to keep the peace at home. John was not a 'mixer' and refused to meet her friends.

When John was stricken with Cancer, Mary took good care of him with never a complaint. She visited him everyday when he was hospitalized. She was never bitter, never melancholy. She never let anyone know when she was 'down'. Mary shared her history with me displaying no animosity. She lived through bad times with the same grace as the good.

She believed in God and was never angry at the hand that life had dealt her.

MARY'S CHARISM

When I am feeling particularly 'ugly', I think of Mary. I picture a little girl dressed in a pretty pink ruffled dress, wearing Mary Jane shoes and white lace trimmed socks, twisting her long curls with her fingers, standing nervously in front of prospective parents - never chosen. Then I envision her as I knew her, with a bright bow in her hair, a self-confident smile on her face, and sharing encouraging words with those around her.

Mary taught me that, although we all have problems, we need not be consumed by misery. Mary's heirloom, her charism, for me is threefold:

- I can endure the sorrows that life deals out;
- always wear a smile;
- and most importantly, always share kind words with others.

Many episodes in my life have been distressing, as they are in everyone's life, but Mary's spirit lives on in me and gives me strength to get through the minor and the major disappointments.

"So we do not lose heart. Even though our outer nature is wasting away, our inner nature is being renewed day by day."

2 Corinthians 4:16

ESTHER

*"One doesn't just become a grouchy old lady;
one was likely a grouchy young lady."*
Jean Riise Leffler

Esther was tall and agile for her age of 70. She was not visibly affected by arthritis, as evidenced by her strong gait and her ability to easily step off the senior transportation van. Her hair was sandy colored, showing little grey, thick and naturally wavy – the kind of hair that other women envy. Her face bore few wrinkles and her hands were so smooth she could have modeled for hand lotion commercials. She was attractive. Esther's countenance was a whole 'nother matter - if ever there was a curmudgeon, it was Esther.

Esther was a 'native daughter' of Shelbyville. She had married her high school sweetheart. He had provided a comfortable life for Esther and their daughter. She had been a home-maker. She worked a garden, kept a spotless home, and was reportedly a good cook. Her husband was her only interest in life after their daughter left for college and set out on her own.

Her life sounds like the idyllic, American dream. But Esther struggled with depression in the days before effective anti-depressant drugs. Esther was as happy as a pessimist personality could be.

I did not know Esther until after a devastating event changed her life. As their 50th wedding anniversary approached, Esther was making plans for a celebration party. Esther's husband had other plans and he served her with divorce papers. No doubt, he had grown tired of dealing with her depressive episodes. He had been bitten by the proverbial 'mid-life crisis.' Adding insult and injury to her embarrassment, Esther's 'replacement' was young, vivacious and beautiful. As a depressive personality, that threw Esther into a deep funk. That was when I met her. Sadly, I cannot remember her ever smiling!

Esther would visit the senior center everyday. Prior to her daily arrival there was a happy buzz around the place. As she entered the door, a hush came over the place. There was a grey cloud over her head and it seemed that Esther loved to share the gloom that consumed her.

In those days before the invention of the internet, I did some research: I read articles, I observed the techniques of my minister, and recalled those of others I had known. About the time Esther was spreading her melancholy I had the privilege of attending a motivational workshop by well known foot ball coach Lou Holtz. In the lecture, he pointed out that negativity was contagious and gave some pointers on how to turn the tide.

Taking it all to heart, I was determined to try to change the atmosphere of the senior center. I enlisted the help of pre-selected seniors. We practiced examples of the 'negative entry' and the opposite 'positive entry' scenarios. I set up a special activity time, serving refreshments (if you feed them they will come!), and began to share my newly acquired wisdom. Using questions I fished for the comments we had rehearsed. As a visual I produced a mini-trash can and gave directions for its use. I called my plan, 'Leave It in the Can'.

The mini-trash can was placed on the traditional sign-in pedestal. The seniors were instructed to come in the door, sign-in and place their complaints and grumbles in the mini-trash can. They were to police the atmosphere themselves, reminding each other that grey clouds were not allowed.

ESTHER'S CHARISM

My 'Leave It in the Can' plan worked - for a while. The mini-trash can remained on the sign-in pedestal; though it appeared empty, it was full of everybody's negativity. Even Esther's! I checked it every day after the people left. Somehow I expected notes. No notes but one day I found a $10.00 bill! It seemed that after the money appeared the negativity seeped back in. Eventually, the technique no longer worked and Esther's grey cloud returned.

Esther's charism? She reinforced something that I already knew; nobody likes to be around a Negative Nellie. I've worked with and for several negative people since Esther's grey cloud entered my life. I have had to work hard within myself to avoid getting caught up in the 'negativity disease' and its close contagious cousin – gossip.

The most important charism I received in knowing Esther is the realization that, 'I cannot purposely change anyone else but I do have the power to permanently change myself!' Some people are comfortable in their misery; they seldom want to change. Because of Esther's example, I work hard to prohibit grey clouds in my comfort zone. I avoid the contamination of Negative Nellie by avoiding <u>her</u>!

"For there is hope for a tree, if it is cut down, that it will sprout again…
Though its root grows old in the earth, and its stump dies in the ground,
yet at the scent of water it will bud and put forth branches like a young
plant."

Job 14:7-9

FRANCES

"Every man's memory is his private literature!"
Aldous Huxley

Meet a hard worker; Frances was a part-time paid worker but a full time un-paid supporter of the senior agency – volunteer extraordinaire. She worked tirelessly despite her apparent fragility.

She didn't have much grey in her natural wavy hair cut in a short pixy 'do' that flattered her small frame. Frances' steps were slow and she appeared unsteady on her feet. Frances proved that looks are often deceiving; she was rather like the egg-shaped Weeble toy. Remember? "Weebles wobble but they don't fall down." She was born, grew up, and grew old in the same small town that her parents had helped settle. She traveled the world – through her reading habit.

Frances and her husband farmed for a living. Her marriage was not particularly happy but she never complained. After her husband died, Frances sold the farm and moved to a small house just inside the city limits. The love for the soil never left her. Frances worked in her yard on weekends, keeping the lawn dandelion free. Her vegetable / herb garden was the only one in town that didn't have any weeds! She didn't preserve her beautiful vegetables for the winter but shared the excess freshness with friends and neighbors.

Two days a week Frances visited the homebound, delivering groceries and prescription refills – that was her paid part-time job. Frances was a welcome visitor who brought news of the 'outside world' for many. Frances spent the other three days on her volunteer 'job' tasks which included recruiting and organizing a corps of other senior volunteers. She knew everyone in town who was over 65 and called on everyone to help in the center's volunteer needs. She was not willing to listen to anyone's lament of being bored at home. She supervised a volunteer crew in stapling, folding, addressing, and mailing the center's newsletter. This was an all day affair which Frances took seriously – she would, literally, not sit down until the last newsletter was delivered to the post office.

After church on Sundays, Frances would drive her vintage 1977, jade green Impala the few short blocks from home to the county museum. As a docent she greeted visitors and conducted tours. Because her family had been among the town's founders, she was able to mix local history with first hand experience. She enjoyed the children's visits and their willingness to hear about the 'olden days.' When there was a special event, Frances helped spread the word by selling tickets. Though she had to be frugal on her tight budget she often bought an extra ticket to treat a friend to such events as the annual Christmas Tea.

What Frances did with her Saturdays was the most wonderful gift to the community of elders living in her small town. Though I suspect she was past 75 herself, she always had a soft spot in her heart for those less fortunate than she. (She was very secretive about her age – though I worked with her for years I was not sure how old she was until someone sent me her obituary! I won't tell; her secret is safe with me.) There were two nursing homes in town and Frances visited each, one in the morning and the other in the afternoon. She stopped in to see old friends. She called them her 'always friends,' not wanting them to feel that she was calling them 'old.' She brought cookies from her kitchen and flowers from her garden. She also chatted with new friends that she made while visiting her 'always friends'. The staff looked forward to her visits as much as the residents because she shared her baked goods at the nurses' stations too. God directed man to 'visit the sick' and Frances took His direction very seriously.

At first glance, it seemed that Frances should have been a resident of the nursing home herself. I sometimes worried that she was spending more money on goodies than she could really afford. As I accompanied her on her nursing home visits and watched the reactions of the beneficiaries of her goodwill I changed my mind. People's faces lit up when they saw her. It was a sight to melt anyone's heart.

FRANCES' CHARISM

Frances single handedly kept the local greeting card store in business. Each week she bought a handful of cards to send to her friends on their birthdays, anniversaries, Easter, and other holidays. Being of Irish descent, she of course celebrated St. Patrick's Day with cards to her Irish friends and Irish-wanna-be's. She spent her evenings writing notes and addressing envelopes. She dreaded each raise in postage rates but never stopped this ministry.

When I left the little town and moved across country, it was Frances who kept me in touch with all the 'gossip.' She wrote to me faithfully each week, even if I didn't write back in a timely manner. I really looked forward to those letters and cards. They meant that someone truly cared about me and made time just for me. I saved them all!

I had the opportunity to recycle the legacy that Frances left to me, by returning it to her. She spent the last few years of her life in one of the nursing homes that she had visited so faithfully. Through Frances' example I came to understand that I can give nothing more valuable to anyone than my time and kind words. Frances taught me that. The greeting card industry and the post office have benefitted from Frances' legacy. So have my friends and family. I am following Frances' example as I buy greeting cards in packets of 10 and send them to my 'always friends.' I'm not as diligent as Frances was about visiting the sick but I will get there – I know I will, because Frances left me a great spiritual gift!

"In the same way, every good tree bears good fruit, but the bad tree bears bad fruit. A good tree cannot bear bad fruit, nor can a bad tree bear good fruit. Every tree that does not bear good fruit is cut down and thrown into the fire. Thus you will know them by their fruits."

Matthew 7:17-20

LILLIAN

Meet one of the most colorful senior-citizens that I ever knew. Lillian was a short roly-poly lady; a flashy dresser matched with comfortable but always dressy shoes. She got her hair regularly permed in a tight overall curl. She did not feel dressed without lipstick and rouge. She wore bodacious costume jewelry. Around others, Lillian was the life of the party. She loved to tell entertaining stories on herself. She laughed at herself as she told this story. "I was making a cake real early this morning. It was hot, so I left the front door open to let in the morning breeze. I was just about to put the pans in the oven and I heard this man's voice say 'Good Morning!' I like'd t' die. I dropped down to the floor so whoever it was at the door wouldn't see me. I was baking with nothing on but my apron! I was scared to death 'til I realized the man's voice was on the radio!"

Lillian had served as the matron on the County Farm for years. Her husband, Cliff, managed the farming business while Lillian cooked, cleaned, cared for the indigent residents, and entertained the County Commissioners. Her days were full of responsibility. She was used to telling people what to do and expected it to be done. The farm never ran smoother than when she was the matron. When Cliff's health failed, they retired to town.

Lillian frequently bragged that her birthday was Christmas day. But Christmas was also a hard time for her. Cliff died in December and that depressed her terribly, year-round but more so each Christmas. Lillian dwelt on her losses. She reminisced quite a lot – always negatively.

Lillian and Cliff had an only child, a son. He grew up and became an influential doctor in the big city. His wife, a young socialite, seemed embarrassed by her in-law's humble roots. She never understood Lillian's domineering personality. She and Lillian drew battle lines and the son was torn between the women in his life. His father had obviously been the mediating influence. After Cliff died, the son and Lillian didn't visit much. Then Lillian had a stroke and the decision was made to move her to an apartment near him. Lillian was needy and demanding though she recovered well from the stroke. She called her son at all hours, pulling him away from family, work and social gatherings. His wife was very unhappy. In marriage he had pledged his allegiance to her. To say there was a falling out between mother and son is an understatement. When he left her apartment for the last time it was with a finality that was never mended.

Nieces moved Lillian back to her hometown and commenced taking care of her needs. Lillian visited the local senior center several times a week. She irritated some with her bossy nature. Others loved her stories and laughed with her, and at her. Wherever Lillian went, she was the center of attention because she was impossible to ignore.

The care by friends and relatives lasted as long as possible. Lillian's demanding ways drove most off in disgust. Others stayed around because, despite her faults, she was lovable and gave lots of love in return. Her medicine was costly but she made her budget stretch to include flour and sugar. With those ingredients on hand, she baked pies and cakes to give away to those 'less fortunate'.

Years after her estrangement from her son, Lillian learned of her great grandson's birth by reading the newspaper. Knowing she would never be allowed to see the baby was a real heart break for her. Later a niece told her of her son's stroke and subsequent retirement. She wanted to reach out to him but couldn't. The hurt was too deep and pride was too strong.

LILLIAN'S CHARISM

Knowing Lillian's story gave me the realization of the sad fact that family ties don't always bind. I grew up in a family full of differences. We didn't argue; we discussed. Sometimes we discussed loudly. But we were always able to talk, even if it was strained. I struggled a long time to understand how Lillian and her family could shut each other out so tightly. Then my life took a twist. My family developed a chasm...I finally understood. And that is when I realized the legacy to be found in Lillian's life. I learned the importance of family and that I must forgive, or at best, ignore transgressions. I have the duty, as the mother, the matriarch of the family, to help the others forgive. I must put pride aside, admit committing wrongs, and humbly ask forgiveness. A line, sometimes just a fine thread, of communication kept open does wonders because we have nothing if we don't have family. Lillian's is a hard charism to live up to but I am thankful that she shared her life's lessons with me.

"Remind them of this, and warn them before God that they are to avoid wrangling over words, which does no good but only ruins those who are listening."
2 Timothy 2:14

FLORENCE

"Fortunate are those who enjoy old age."

Jewish Proverb

Do you remember Estelle Getty? She played Sophia in the sit-com, Golden Girls. In real-life she was the youngest of the actresses though she played Bea Arthur's mother. Ms. Getty studied the aged in 'their natural setting' before taking the part. That preliminary work is what made Sophia so believable as an elderly woman who had survived a stroke.

Estelle Getty was a presenter at a state conference on aging. She was very short and had to stand on a stool to be seen over the podium. Florence and I had the opportunity to meet Ms. Getty at that conference. It seemed that Ms. Getty was more excited to meet Florence than Florence was to meet her because Florence was shorter than Estelle Getty!

Florence, too, was short; however she was one of the strongest women I have ever known. Florence was crippled by arthritis years before I met her. Her fingers were perpendicular to her palm. She walked with a cane, lovingly handmade by her husband Kenneth. Their lovely turn of the century two story home was retro-fitted with a stair/chair lift so Florence could still reach the upstairs bedroom. She painstakingly typed her frequent correspondence on a typewriter. She frequently wrote to state and federal legislators to share her opinions on proposals that affected the elderly. She cooked nutritious meals for Kenneth who was newly diagnosed with diabetes. In addition, she kept herself busy with community activities.

Florence had snow-white wavy hair, arranged in an old-fashioned Mary Pickford style. Her complexion was flawless – soft with few wrinkles. Her kindness and grace shone in her smile. It is no wonder that she had been voted the state senior queen a few years before I met her. During 'Florence's year', she and Kenneth had travelled the state to a year-long flurry of events that year. It seemed that everywhere she went she was given a corsage of silk flowers. She had one to match every outfit she wore.

By the time I met Florence, she and Kenneth were slowing down some. For instance, they cut back on their involvement with the Area Agency on Aging – they still volunteered at the county level but that was considerably less than their prior commitments at the state level! They had begun to attend the senior center regularly but once a week was all they could find time for!

It is said, 'pride goeth before the fall' and many people in need of support are too prideful to use a cane when they decline. Not Florence. She was not prideful, unless you classify being well dressed with perfectly applied make-up and coifed hair, prideful. Florence was not self-conscious about using her cane; especially because Kenneth had made for her. You see, Kenneth had adapted her special cane to 'wear' her corsage mementos. That was recycling at its very best; she had an outfit to go with every corsage!

FLORENCE'S CHARISM

Florence's lessons were two-fold:

I loved to visit Florence in her historic home. She had such a positive outlook on life. She rarely gave advice instead she shared her suggestions through stories.

When I was discouraged over my daughters' poor life choices Florence told me of her son-in-law's decision not to finish college. He was more than half way through when he dropped out. He and Florence's daughter were going to 'travel the world' for a while and 'find themselves.' Needless to say, that was a great disappointment to Florence and Kenneth. They were worried about the 'kids' on many levels. Rather than react badly, Florence shared with me her advice to the young couple; she did not care if they became ditch diggers as long as they were the best darn ditch diggers they could possibly be. She had taught her daughter a good work ethic and prayed that she had also influenced her son-in-law. Florence helped me to understand that my own daughters' life choices were theirs to make. I encouraged them to be the best darn 'ditch digger that they could possibly be'. I tried to imitate Florence's example. I came close, I worried and prayed, but I did not interfere – too much.

Secondly:

I resolved that should I ever be in need of assistance I would not be prideful. Florence epitomized the author, Barbara Johnson's philosophy. The title of her book exemplified Florence's life, *Pain Is Inevitable, Misery Is Optional, So Stick a Geranium in Your Hat and Be Happy!* As my own 'golden years' approach I use a cane occasionally when walking great distances or across unpaved parking lots. Though I don't have a corsage to match every outfit, my husband has attached hiking medallions to my cane. My cane is now a memento of state and national parks which we have visited over the years. Just as Florence's corsage decorated cane displayed her spirit, my medallion decorated cane displays my spirit; I am always ready for a new place to explore!

"The might of your awesome deeds shall be proclaimed, and I will declare your greatness. They shall celebrate the fame of your abundant goodness and shall sing aloud of your righteousness."

Psalm 145:6-7

MAC AND LELA

"To see a young couple loving each other is no wonder, but to see an old couple an old couple loving each other is the best sight of all."
William Makepeace Thackery

These were two of my most favorite people at the senior center. Because we lived states away from blood family, they became surrogate grand-parents to my two daughters. I can't wait for you to meet them!

Mac bought their first house shortly after he married Lela. He loved to tell the story; "the house belonged to an old lady. It needed some work and she couldn't afford to have it done. She was going to live with her daughter. We didn't have any money but I was able to borrow the $1,300 I needed to cover the price." Lela would pick up the story from there; "I was so upset at going into debt. $1,300 was a lot of money in 1935 and I just knew we couldn't pay it back."

About a year later, after doing the repairs, Mac and Lela sold that first home at the tidy sum of $1,800 - a $500 profit! Lela felt better. $500 Was a great return on their investment. As time progressed, they bought, lived in, fixed up, and sold other houses. Each time they bought a house, Lela became less fearful and each time they sold a house, she became more confident in their future.

Mac was drafted into the Army at the beginning of World War II. He was wounded in action while serving in Europe. Rather than being sent home to recuperate, he was given a desk job in an engineering office. A general recognized Mac's potential and counseled him to take advantage of the GI Bill when he got home. Mac did just that. Soon after his Army discharge Mac studied to become a master plumber. He opened a business and was the best in town. He won national recognition for his problem solving skills and engineering know-how. All the while, he and Lela bought, lived in, fixed up, and sold houses. The shortest time they lived in one house was four months and the longest was four years. Lela often said "I agreed to move so often to avoid spring cleaning!"

37

When I got to know Mac, he was bald on top with beautiful snow white hair encircling his head just above his ears. He wore wire rimmed glasses that could not hide his dancing blue eyes. Age made him fragile. He walked with a shuffle because of tiring knees. His hips pained him too, especially during the harsh Midwestern winters. He was little in stature, but his spirit and heart were as big as Montana!

Mac's life-long hobby was clowning. Lela painted his face with the expertise of an accomplished artist. Mac donned the colorful suit, funny shoes and bright yellow wig, with a bee in it, and he *BECAME* Mac-a-roni. When Mac was forced to wear a hearing aid he learned he could cup his hand over his ear and make the hearing aid whistle. Taking advantage, he would call a child close and whisper, "listen." Cupping his hand, he created the whistle and told the child his bee was talking. This little trick never ceased to amaze the youngsters and Mac loved to see the little ones jump. When Mac got too frail to march in the local parades, he rode his bike, later a motorbike, and still later in a convertible. He would never let the parade pass Mac-a-roni by!

Mac and Lela came to the senior center every day. They didn't need the meal provided there because Lela was a great cook. In fact, because of their years of successful real estate investments, they could afford to eat at local restaurants every day. They came because they enjoyed the fellowship. They came early and greeted the others, often getting coffee for those more frail than themselves. They served as good-will ambassadors for the senior program.

MAC'S CHARISM

There were times when Mac's hearing loss appeared to isolate him. The din at the senior center bothered him. I often found him sitting alone at the far back table (it was quieter there). As often as I could, I made the time to sit down and visit with him. He told me the story of the Army general many times. I listened each time as if it were the first time I heard it. Then Mac would give me encouraging words about myself and my future. I would smile and nod at the appropriate times. He didn't have to hear me, but I'm sure glad that I heard him!

Mac shared his philosophies of life with me often. He encouraged my husband and me to continue our home remodeling efforts (at that point we were working on our fourth remodel). Mac saw a potential in me for which I had never even looked. He helped me to know myself better.

Mac's lesson was to instill in me the drive to be the best that I can be. I still strive to live up to that instruction. I would like to do better, to be better, but I do my best – and in that way I am living up to the Mac's spirit.

"... husbands should love their wives as they do their own bodies. He who loves his wife loves himself."

Ephesians 5:4

LELA AND MAC

"In love, as in other matters, the young are just beginners."
Isaac Bashevis Singer

You've gotten to know Mac, now I want you to know Lela better. Lela was a short woman with a spine crooked from osteoporosis. Her hair had a hint of silvery-blue that highlighted her bright blue eyes. She always wore an antique locket on a long gold chain. A loose fitting, gold engagement and wedding ring set adorned her arthritic ring finger. Her elastic banded watch was nothing special. She was a spiffy dresser but not over the top. She wore relaxed, bright clothes and comfortable, stylish shoes. She often said she was glad to be alive in the 1990's so she didn't have to wear gloves and hats anymore!

While Lela and Mac were buying, living in, fixing up and selling houses, there was a deep sorrow in Lela's life. Their marriage was strong but something was missing. Lela wanted a baby, desperately. They were not so blessed.

In time, Mac learned of an infant through their minister, a boy, rejected by his mother at birth. Foster parenting was very informal in the early days of their marriage. Mac told Lela of this baby and her heart leapt with hope. They took him in and this child made their family complete. Mac and Lela were very happy. They raised the boy to about 18 months old. At that time they filed papers to legally adopt him. At the last minute in the adoption process the boy's biological mother re-entered the picture and demanded the boy be returned to her. Lela and Mac were devastated.

Sixty-plus years after the heart wrenching separation, Lela still grieved. Though she told me this story more than once, she never told me the baby's name. She always choked back tears and referred to him only as "the boy." The heartbreak never healed.

In her later years, Lela had several heart attacks. She underwent heart surgery and a strenuous rehab program. After her Monday rehab session she would drag herself to the senior center and swear she would never go back. On Tuesday, her day off, she felt a little better, a little stronger, and agreed to go back on Wednesday. On Wednesday, she would once again drag herself to the senior center and again vow she was never going back to rehab. Thursday was better and she would actually plan on going again on Friday. Friday found her dragging again but this time she knew she had two days off and didn't even talk about not going back to rehab on Monday. And so it went, for four weeks. Lela stuck it out. She hated every minute of it but she kept working, and she got better. Though her body was tired, she never faltered in her attitude. Two months later, on the day after the Super Bowl, when she was 84, I announced that we should have a Super Bowl Party the next year. Lela exclaimed, "I'll bring the ham!"

LELA'S CHARISM

Lela's spiritual legacy is an observation. Heart trouble is inevitable. For some it is emotional heart trouble, like Lela's lost baby ordeal. For some it is physical heart trouble, like Lela's heart attacks, surgery and rehab. No one escapes. The attitude during rehab, be it physical, emotional or spiritual, determines the outcome.

These days when I have a heavy heart over an emotional issue I think back on Lela's outlook. My own physical heart trouble has not been as severe as Lela's but I search deep for the level of grit Lela exhibited. Through her heart troubles, Lela taught me to keep going, work hard, look to the future and make plans with hope and confidence.

Lela's inner soul can be summed up in her statement –"I'll bring the ham!"

"Each of you, however, should love his wife as himself, and a wife should respect her husband."

Ephesians 5:33

LEW AND PAULINE

"I am still a man in progress."

Billy Graham

Let me introduce you to Lew and his wife, Pauline. I only met her once but I worked with Lew often and came to admire him – a lot.

Pauline had a brain disease that incapacitated her while she was in her fifties. By the time she was 65, Pauline was a total-care invalid who could do or say little. Lew kept her at home, hiring help so he could get out for groceries and have a few hours of socialization each week. Taking care of Pauline around the clock took its toll. The house deteriorated as Lew's time and energy were spent feeding, changing and bathing Pauline. Their only son lived 25 miles away and wasn't able to visit often. Lew's brothers and sisters lived in other states. It was a lonely life for Lew. He knew he had to make some changes for his sake as well as Pauline's. The time came for nursing home placement. It was a heart wrenching decision for Lew. In the end, Pauline didn't even recognize the change.

As Pauline was settled in at the nursing home, Lew knew he had to find a way to spend his time. He was a strapping, healthy 72 year-old with the potential for many active years ahead. He exercised daily by walking to the senior center. He came to the center to volunteer. Lew offered to help any way he could. He helped serve lunch at the center every day. Being a retired carpenter, he worked in the center's wood shop, making items to sell in the center's little gift shop. He was not afraid of big city traffic and soon he was driving elderly clients to doctor and hospital appointments in the neighboring county. He came early and stayed late at every fund raiser throughout the calendar year. He was honored as 'Volunteer of the Year' more than once. Through all the volunteerism, Lew went faithfully, everyday, to see Pauline at the nursing home. On good days, Pauline would exhibit a small reaction to his presence. Most days, sadly, she didn't even know he was there. At night Lew was home alone with the TV.

Lew befriended two particular ladies. One loved to cook and would invite Lew over for supper. She was about ten years older than he was. It was a platonic friendship that fulfilled both's need for companionship. Lew took her to the grocery story, the doctor, the pharmacy, and the discount store whenever she asked. They argued politics often. She was a strong liberal Democrat and he, a strong conservative Republican. Sometimes the arguments would result in Lew leaving and not returning for weeks on end. He would laugh and tell me, "When she apologizes for calling me a damn-Republican, I'll go back."

The other lady was about the same age as Lew. They were so good for one another and I found myself wishing that Lew was free to marry her. This platonic friendship was a beautiful relationship. They laughed easily together. They went out to eat, and to the movies; they were traveling companions on group trips – always taking separate rooms. It was bittersweet to watch this friendship blossom.

Lew gave of himself to everyone he met. He was always helping someone in need. He gave, he helped, he worked, and he went – like the Energizer Bunny - until he would sit down in front of the TV at night and fall asleep from exhaustion, still in his clothes.

The last time I saw Lew was at a mutual friend's funeral. He stood near the casket, away from the other mourners, tears quietly streaming down his cheeks. I went over and hugged him. He told me, "I'm going to keep going until I die." And he did. One morning over coffee, while making plans to take someone to the city, Lew had a fatal heart attack. Pauline never knew he was gone.

Lew could have been more selfish in his life. He could have divorced Pauline and few would have thought ill of him. Instead, he abided by his marriage vows. He gave of himself every waking minute and always included his invalid wife in his daily travels. He kept busy, planning the day, the week, and the errands.

LEW'S CHARISM

Lew taught me the importance of dedicated, unselfish love. Lew's spiritual lesson to me was to be true to those who depend on me – keep my promises. Never forget that marriage is for better or worse, sickness and health, until death do we part. On days that I feel pulled in six different directions by family, job, and volunteer obligations, I think of Lew's last words to me. I resolve that I, too, am going to "keep going until I die!"

"From the fig tree learn its lesson: as soon as its branch becomes tender and puts forth its leaves, you know that summer is near. So also, when you see all these things, you know that he is near, at the very gates. Truly I tell you, this generation will not pass away until all these things have taken place. Heaven and earth will pass away, but my words will not pass away."
Matthew 24:32-35

LORRAINE

"If wrinkles must be written upon our brows, let them not be written on our heart. The spirit should never grow old."

James A. Garfield

Lorraine had three children, all in school but still young, when she was stricken with crippling arthritis. It was so bad that she was wheel chair bound for a while. Doctors told her that she would never walk again. Lorraine didn't accept that and set about being busy. Despite the pain that 'old man Arthur Itis' induced, Lorraine taught herself to knit and crochet. She worked her fingers until she couldn't stand the pain anymore. She would rest, then work some more. Over time her fingers limbered up and the pain caused by the movement eased too.

Walking was painful and done in the house at first. She worked at each step. With time she was walking with a cane out on the sidewalk. She made herself walk the kids to school. She improved a little each week and eventually Lorraine was walking independently.

Lorraine knew that she would regress to the crippled stage quickly with inactivity. Thus started a lifetime of handwork and helping others. She got active with her church women's group, the hospital volunteer 'pink ladies,' and the PTA. If someone needed something sewn, mended or quilted they brought it to Lorraine.

As her children grew and left home, Lorraine became active at the town's library. She was patient and loving during story time. She was creative, often making and working puppets for shows. There was a lot of child in her. She loved to play! Her enthusiasm for books and children even inspired one of her grandsons to major in Library Science in college. She was so proud to volunteer for his programs at the library.

I met Lorraine just after he husband died. They had been very close. It was a terrible blow for her. She cried, she was angry; she experienced all the usual stages of grief. She participated in a grief workshop held at the senior center. Then she picked herself up and set about being busy and began to participate in life again.

And participate she did! Lorraine shared her handwork knowledge with many people. She was a fixture at the community annual Pioneer Festival, teaching quilting to young and old. She belonged to a craft club that met monthly. If she wasn't teaching, she was learning something new to teach someone else!

For years, Lorraine sewed toys for the children going through the emergency room, lab or x-ray departments at the local hospital. After her husband died she moved the project to the senior center to get others involved in life. Her toy project gave many of her fellow-seniors a reason to get up in the morning. A group of women, and even men, met weekly to cut out, stitch, stuff and name cloth animals to deliver to the hospital. They made a minimum of 25 toys each week all year 'round. As Lorraine aged and her health began to fail her she was forced to move to a retirement community close to her son. She left the senior center but she left behind an ongoing toy project that continued for years.

Many agencies honored Lorraine for her volunteerism. She was a great example of the spirit of giving. Lorraine's giving touched so many lives, from museum and library visitors to the kids at the hospital, to her fellow seniors at the center. Lorraine taught me to quilt. I watched her tat, but I could never get the hang of that. She taught me that one is never too old to master a new skill nor too old to volunteer!

LORRAINE'S CHARISM

I still have a doll that Lorraine made for me. It is a small cloth doll with a gingham dress and a coordinating quilted blanket. It is all hand stitched. As I feel the aches of arthritis creeping into my body, I think of Lorraine keeping her fingers limber by sewing that doll for me. I know that she gave me more than just a doll. Lorraine gave me the conviction that pain can be conquered. Lorraine knew that doctors don't always get it right. Without pain, there is no gain and without Lorraine's example, I might not have discovered that on my own.

"Lift up your hands to the holy place, and bless the Lord."

Psalms 134:2

PAUL

"If I had known I would live this long, I would have taken better care of myself."

H.J. Springston

Meet Paul, a drinker who started early and practiced the habit most of his life. He joined the Army and fought in the South Pacific during World War II. He did not reminisce about that period in his life often, but when he did, he got choked up. It was obvious that combat left a profound impression on him. His were not physical scars but emotional ones. He came home safe but habitually drinking. He may have suffered Post Traumatic Stress Disorder before the effects of war was given a title. He drifted from job to job and bottle to bottle. He married Goldie and they had a daughter. He couldn't hold onto a job or his marriage due to his drinking. Though he worked for the rail road for a few years, long enough to get a small pension, he never had a 'good' job for very long. His Social Security was a pittance. Alcohol consumed him well into his retirement years.

Paul, over six feet tall and obviously undernourished, came to the senior center to eat the government subsidized meals because he couldn't afford to buy groceries. He was not much of a cook anyway. He was disheveled and sometimes unruly. Others cringed when he came in the door. Though he was friendly and spoke to everyone, most tried to avoid him.

When Paul turned 70-something, he showed signs of heart trouble. That gave him cause to take a long, hard look at his life. He came to realize that it was up to him, and only him, to stop drinking or face the Grim Reaper in a short time. He chose the bumpier path and quit drinking.

Paul worked hard, harder than ever before, to quit drinking. He made his life change without help from Alcoholics Anonymous. *HE* did it – with God's help. He continued to come to the senior center daily for the food. As word of his sobriety spread, people visited with him more. There was still some whispering behind his back but he held his head high and ignored it. The gossip faded over time along with the drunken image Paul had once projected.

Paul grew into the role of volunteer at the senior center. He became the best Bingo caller. He took that 'job' seriously, often plotting and planning new ways to make the game more challenging for the players. He recruited others to help set up the prize table. He would call Bingo for two hours straight with a cup of coffee at his elbow.

His new friends introduced Paul to the art of clowning and helped to create a new character. Mac gave him an old wig. Lorraine made him a clown costume. Lela painted his happy face. All clowns have a name and because he hung out with Mac-a-roni, he became Mr. Cheese. He wasn't a silent clown; Paul didn't know how to be silent! He wasn't strong enough to march in the local festival parade so he fixed up an old motor scooter and rode it in a criss cross path tossing out candy to the children along the route. His smile was a broad as the avenue! This image made his personal transformation complete.

PAUL'S CHARISM

I learned a lot from Paul. Of course, he taught me a variety of Bingo games. More importantly, he taught me that an old dog *can* learn new tricks. He taught me to put a smile on my face even it is just painted on.

Paul's family said that he never amounted to much. I know better. He beat his lifelong addiction. Paul's charism is the conviction that I hold to this day - it is never too late to change.

LOURENE

"You can't help getting older, but you don't have to get old."
George Burns

I want you to meet one very involved senior, Lourene. At 80-something, she was slender, nimble, strong, and weatherworn from a life time of being a farmer. Despite her age she loved to have fun. She often told jokes, but never at anyone else's expense. Lourene was a giver – always ready to help others. In her retirement, she did not slow down; she simply redirected her energy to help the senior center in its fundraising efforts. Lourene was game for involvement no matter what the need.

Shelbyville's city circle is a favorite spot for evening concerts, town festivals, and community events. While I worked there, the senior center presented the annual Strawberry Festival on the third Friday of June. We planned for any contingency, including the unpredictable weather. That's why we set up heavy-duty commercial tents to protect us from the sun or rain. In the early morning hours of June 1991, the skies were cloudy and promised rain. I was glad we had set up two tents, end to end, that year.

Our fund-raising was important to the senior center budget. To the staff, fund-raising was a necessary chore. But to the seniors, fund-raising took on a social atmosphere. Men and women gladly signed up to help. This was the first outdoor event of the summer and was traditionally well attended by the townspeople. We were all committed and excited – expecting a good outcome and income. Most of the seniors we had recruited to work were unconcerned by weather reports; they had grown up with the unpredictable Midwestern spring weather. Nevertheless Strawberry Festival Day, as we called, progressed with great anticipation.

Lourene was scheduled to unpack homemade yellow sheet cakes, slice them, place the slices in checkered cardboard boat bowls and keep two serving lines supplied with cake. This was not a simple task, as we were known to serve more than 800 strawberry shortcakes in just three hours! Lourene and the other volunteers donned matching red bib aprons over their white shirts and worked feverishly as the customers began to line up. They looked festive for sure!

About half way through the festival one of our customers whispered some disconcerting news to me - we were under severe storm warnings. The person did not want to alarm the workers or the customers. The sky didn't look overly threatening, but the store buildings around the circle blocked my wider view. The Midwestern weather changed quickly that day.

It began with a sudden squall lifting a corner tent pole off the ground, up and over one of the serving tables. Supplies went sailing. A senior volunteer and I struggled to right the leg while Lourene kept her cool and began to stack the cakes into cardboard crates to protect them from the impending rain.

The next blast of wind brought an instantaneous deluge. The tent pole we were still struggling with was ripped from our hands and the tent blew down. The cakes Lourene was trying to protect sailed across the parking lot by the tempest. Instantly everyone was soaked!

People ran for cover into nearby parked cars and the stores rimming the circle. In the confusion a little girl, about five years old, got separated from her mother and took cover under one of our abandoned serving tables. Her mother thought she was right behind her as she pushed her younger child's stroller to safety into a store across the street.

Lourene found the little girl while on her own way to safety; she bent down and introduced herself to the little girl and calmly took the girl by the hand. The wind was blowing and it was raining hard. Lourene hurried them both to the back of her full sized blue and white pickup truck. Lourene opened the camper shell hatch. She lifted the little girl into the truck then climbed over the tailgate herself. Despite her nimbleness, at 80-something it had to be difficult for Lourene's five-foot five-inch frame to load them both into the bed of the big old truck. I know it was a struggle to close the hatch in the surging wind and driving rain, but emergencies often bring out super human strength. That was Lourene – Super Woman.

The rain and wind grew nastier. The tents were completely down and ripping against their metal framework. Whole cakes were blown across town – probably to the next county! Debris was everywhere. And the little girl was terrified. She sat in the bed of Lourene's pick up truck, sobbing. I can only imagine her mother's terror when she reached shelter in the store and realized her daughter wasn't with her.

Fear gripped the little girl but if Lourene was scared she never let the little girl know. Instead, Lourene soothingly prayed a prayer for safety then coaxed the girl to sing with her. Though Lourene had never had children her motherly instinct was strong. And she knew that fear is often overcome by song. Lourene had to think fast and quite fittingly the first song she thought was Row, Row, Row Your Boat! The storm raged, the truck rocked in the wind and they sang Rock A Bye Baby. Befitting the circumstances, Lourene taught her the Itsy-Bitsy Spider finger-play song. In time, the little girl barely noticed the storm because she was having fun with Lourene.

Then, as quickly as the wind picked up the tent, the wind died. It rained for a few more minutes and then stopped. People began to emerge from their shelters like turtles peeking out of their shells. Everyone looked up first, scanning the skies, and then they surveyed the area. The town's center was strewn with Strawberry Festival debris - and *all* of it was wet. The plastic tablecloths that had covered the serving line tables were shredded. Only one corner of the two commercial tents was left standing.

City agency workers seemed to appear from nowhere! Garbage trucks brought a clean-up crew. Policemen checked on the senior volunteers. Paramedics treated minor injuries. Two were taken to the hospital.

Lourene opened the camper hatch easily in the storm's aftermath. She could see a woman pushing a stroller frantically around the parking lot and calling a girl's name. Super woman,

Lourene, climbed out of the truck and made herself heard over the noise of the sirens, garbage trucks and city staff barking orders. Recognition brought tears of gratitude as the frantic mother raced to Lourene's truck. The woman peered into the sanctuary to find her little girl, still wet but smiling. It took Super Woman and mom both to lift the little girl over the truck's tail gate – Lourene's Super Woman strength was spent. Mom was reunited with her little girl.

LOURENE'S CHARISM

The whole storm wreaked its havoc in less than 15 minutes. With the city's help, the debris was cleaned up in another 15 minutes. After my own trip to the hospital, I found Lourene back at the senior center helping to restore order there. We salvaged what we could, and sold off the remaining strawberries – without cake. Our fund raising income was greatly reduced that year but the lessons Lourene taught me that day have lasted my lifetime:

- Storms in life are inevitable - take cover.
- Don't let fear paralyze you - if we keep our wits, we can deal with whatever comes.
- Oh yes, one more thing, it doesn't hurt to sing a happy song.

"For there is hope for a tree, if it is cut down, that it will sprout again..."

Job 14:7

52

ANNA

"Beauty comes in all ages, colors, shapes, and forms. God never makes junk."

Kathy Ireland

Anna had a baby and raised her without benefit of a marriage during a time when that was scandalous. She was strong-willed and strong-backed. She worked hard to provide a simple life for her and her daughter. They had to watch every penny to make ends meet. She was often the object of harassment by male bosses and gossip by the "proper ladies" in town. She didn't socialize much and had few friends. She was always careful to shield her daughter from the whispering.

After her daughter married and left home, Anna continued to work. She was frugal and eventually was able to buy a duplex with the plan of living in one half and renting the other thereby providing for her retirement. Both halves needed work. With no money for expensive repairmen, Anna learned carpentry, painting and other handyman tasks. She lived like a monk with a modicum of furniture and conveniences. She didn't have a TV so she read books borrowed from the library. She shopped at thrift stores. The cashiers at the bakery surplus store knew her by name.

Anna lived a solitary life. In the evening after painting walls, or fixing a stuck window, she would sit at her modest kitchen table making rosaries for the church. When she was conserving bright light bulbs Anna would crochet lap robes for the local nursing home residents – she was expert enough to do that blindfolded! It had always been Anna against the world and her retirement years would be no different.

Anna came to the senior center on Wednesdays to participate in the toy making project. Some of the other seniors were still stand-off-ish, remembering and still judging Anna for the indiscretion of her youth. As she always had, Anna held her head high and participated with her fine sewing talents.

Bob, a recent widower came to the center to lift the curtain of his sadness. Bob, a successful farmer, was always industrious and became involved in the men's woodshop. His wife's illness and death had been a long ordeal. He was really suffering from loneliness.

Bob met Anna on a Wednesday. They chatted easily from the first moment they met. Soon they were both coming several days a week. They became good friends and soon their friendship blossomed into courtship. One day Anna came to me and held up her left hand – on her third finger was a shiny unpretentious engagement ring! Anna was glowing. It was evident that Bob gained a new lease on life.

There were a few 'snipers' who continued to whisper behind Anna's back. They hissed that Bob's first wife was hardly cold yet. Bob and Anna ignored it all with grace and dignity. It was wonderful to watch two 70-something year olds fall in love. Nothing and no one was going to hurt them because they found each other! I was there when they 'tied the knot' on the eleventh day of the eleventh month at the eleventh hour – that is the way they announced the wedding. It was a dignified quiet ceremony.

Anna and her new husband worked together on Bob's farm. They took care of newborn piglets when the sow died. They planted a garden and put up the surplus for the harsh Midwestern winter. They took long walks holding hands in the evenings. They sold her duplex and travelled. They were as much in love as two young kids.

As the years progressed, Anna and Bob remained on the farm despite Anna's failing eyesight. She continued to crochet lap robes for the nursing home residents. Bob picked the colors for her. They adapted the old farm house to fit her handicap and she continued to cook and clean with Bob's oversight for her safety.

Anna's physical and emotional strength always impressed me. Macular degeneration only slowed her, it didn't stop her. When she couldn't do something she always had, she found a new way to do it. At 75 years old, Anna told me she wanted to learn Braille so she could read the Bible!

I could tell you that knowing Anna taught me that it is what is inside of you that counts. Despite what others think and say about you, the important thing is: hold your head up, go about your business, work hard and be honest. Those are indeed noble charisms, but they are life lessons we should be able to develop on our own as we grow up if we look to good examples.

Anna's spirit encourages me to trust that fairy tales do come true. There is a bit of advice I want to pass along to you: when Prince Charming sneaks into your life, say yes! Anna taught me that we can indeed "live happily ever after".

"Now in the fifteenth day of the seventh month, when you have gathered the produce of the land, you shall keep the festival of the Lord...on the first day you shall take the fruit of majestic trees, branches of palm trees, boughs of leafy trees, and willows of the brook; and you shall rejoice before the Lord your God for seven days."

Leviticus 23:39-40

JOHN AND PEG

"The secret of genius is to carry the spirit of the child into old age, which means never losing your enthusiasm."

Aldous Huxley

Both widowed while in their late twenties, John and Peg paid their 'dues' as single parents at a time when there was little social service support available. Neither of them was looking for a long-term relationship when they met at a church function. Their children were friends at school - both public school and Sunday school. John and Peg became close and fell deeply in love. After their marriage John and Peg considered having a child together but decided their family was complete. They became a blended family before The Brady Bunch!

The company John worked for offered 'retirement lessons' for their executives. He investigated several hobby activities before settling on throwing class and forming ceramic bowls, cups, and vases on the pottery wheel. He took that art a step further and developed his own formulas for glazes. He held pottery classes for children and adults in his garage. He and Peg took his finished pieces to craft shows around central Indiana. Peg was always frustrated by browsers' comments of, "why should I pay $7.00 for your bowl when I can buy a bowl at Wal-Mart for $2.99!?!" Peg tried hard to educate the public.

John's executive position afforded them a comfortable retirement. They were both well educated and well traveled. They enjoyed the culture available in the greater Indianapolis area. They visited museums, attended opening night performances of the ballet and community plays. They were generous with their time and resources. They helped their children if they needed it and volunteered, working tirelessly, for local service agencies.

John and Peg spent their free time together. The devotion between them was commendable – and occasionally an embarrassment. Peg shared this story with me:

"I wanted a new dress to wear to an art exhibit so John drove me to the mall. I chose four dresses to try on. I left John sitting on a 'husband chair' near the door." Peg said the dressing room was full of women in varying state of dress. She went on, "I was having a grand time trying on outfit after outfit. I was on dress number three when I heard a woman shriek; then another; then an indignant saleswoman demanding, 'sir, you are not allowed in here and I must ask you to leave.'" The saleswoman was scolding John! Peg explained, "I had taken longer than he thought necessary and came to check on me." As Peg related this story to me I was laughing – she was not. Peg did not appreciate John's concern! No, she did not buy any of their dresses and she swore to me that she would never allow him to accompany her shopping again!

Though they didn't go clothes shopping again, John and Peg volunteered together for the Area Agency on Aging. I met the couple just after they helped the senior center attain a grant which had included filing papers to state government, contacting city officials, canvassing the community for signatures, and all under tight time constraints. It was a project suited for a team like these two active seniors. They had jumped in and never looked back. After the grant was awarded, both stayed active on the board of directors for years. There was always a fund raiser to be organized, a new grant to be investigated, and policy changes to be challenged. John and Peg were not only there every step of the way, they were leading the way!

THEIR CHARISMS

John's and Peg's charism is an understanding of the need for planned activity in retirement. Work-a-holism among Americans is a problem addiction. We pack three weeks of activity into a one week vacation; but we don't know how to <u>plan</u> for retirement. Too many reach the end of a long career; get their gold watch; retire, and are miserable – because they retired from life.

John and Peg had a healthy retirement for many reasons. They continued to learn, they continued to teach others, they continued to be involved in life, and they continued to be engaged in their community. They taught me to welcome my own retirement without trepidation. It is never too early to begin to plan for my golden years. That plan involves more than contributing to my 401K; I am investigating causes and agencies to which I will dedicate my free time.

Oh, there is one more thing that they taught me: do not take my husband dress shopping!

"...you must not destroy its trees by wielding an axe against them. Although you may take food from them, you must not cut them down."

Deuteronomy 20:19

LLOYD

"The man who is too old to learn was probably always too old to learn."

Henry S. Haskins

Lloyd had a commanding presence. His entrance in a room almost required one to stand out of respect. His persona was such that people of all ages sat spell bound when he related stories of "the old ways." Lloyd did not dwell on the past but he loved to teach about it. His grandmother had been 'stolen' by an Indian tribe as a child and was raised with the tribe's traditional ways until she was a grown woman. She eventually returned to the white-man's culture and married Lloyd's grandfather. Longevity was in the family genes and both grandparents lived long lives and shared much with Lloyd.

Lloyd was a historical re-enactor all of his adult life. He owned a genuine tee-pee and participated in living history events throughout the Midwest in his youthful days. The long lodge poles became too much to handle in his advancing years and he was relegated to the modern tent camping area of the rendezvous events. That did not deter him; Lloyd continued to dress for the occasion in full buckskin clothing and hunting accoutrements. The fringe on his sleeves and the beads around his neck drew the attention of the young children. His description of hunting methods particularly enthralled the teen boys and their dads. He demonstrated living skills of starting a fire with a flint and steel and cooking over that open fire.

As Lloyd weakened with age and was not comfortable loading his wares, driving across the state, and setting up a camp to dramatize the ancient living skills, Lloyd sent word to the local schools that he was available for living history lessons in the classrooms. He had an annual circuit in the general area. He would dress in his full regalia and tell the story of his grandmother and the pioneers. He shared tales of the hardships and even the recreational games of the old days. He never let a lesson end before imparting the importance of the sacrifice and the courage it took to settle our American land.

Lloyd knew how to tan a hide, rendering it soft and supple; how to make beef jerky; how to make a hunting bow and arrows that would fly straight. He was a master basket weaver. And he was happy to teach these skills to anyone willing to learn.

LLOYD'S CHARISM

Lloyd's charism changed my family! Lloyd loved telling stories, historical in nature. My husband and I, inspired by Lloyd, became rendezvous-ers ourselves and began including our first grandson in our encampment when he was only three. Our granddaughter attended her first rendezvous at the age of one month. It took my husband and me a little longer to gain the courage to bring our twin grandsons to any event that included open fires, but they are a regular fixture now. We are all historical re-enactors, depicting the 1840's. We participate in living history events at our state parks. My husband demonstrates candle-making. Our twin-grandsons teach about the fur trade and encourage the public to identify the fur samples we have accumulated. My teen-aged grandson can start a fire with a flint and steel. My grand-daughter exhibits toys and games of the earlier era. I can usually be found at the center of a group of children learning to make dolls from corn husks.

Lloyd's charism of passing on history affected so many. There is no way of knowing how many history teachers he might have inspired. If they are not teaching in the formal classroom, I am certain that most are bringing their own children to history preservation events.

It is said that we learn from our mistakes. If we don't know *(and admit)* our mistakes we are destined to repeat them. The only way we will avoid repeating our mistakes is to know our past! Lloyd did more than his fair share of correcting our mistakes through his history lessons.

"Not many of you should become teachers, my brothers and sisters, for you know that we who teach will be judged with greater strictness."

James 34:1

ELLEN

"I intend to remain young indefinitely."

Mary Pickford

Note: It is not my practice to use last names in these characterizations, but because Ellen's last name was Young and it is important to her profile, I use it.

Ellen was small in stature with a round friendly and youthful face. Her hair showed little grey and naturally maintained its youthful deep shade of auburn. That had attributed to my immediate ability to remember her name upon our first meeting...Ellen Young.

Ellen moved to Shelbyville when her husband retired from a long career with the Corps of Engineers. As a couple they had moved across the country many times, raising their children in diverse places. When her husband died, Ellen stayed on in town but regularly travelled to visit her five children who themselves had scattered across the country.

Ellen was ready for any challenge and every new adventure. She was a frequent globe-trotter – bus, cruise ship, plane, train... It didn't matter what the mode of transportation was, if someone said, "Let's go" Ellen was packed and ready! One of her favorite places to visit was Colorado. She claimed the sky was as close as the tips of her fingers at the ends of outstretched arms. It helped that one of her daughters and family lived near Denver.

Ellen was never one to be housebound by the weather. When her grandchildren went outside to build a giant snowman, Ellen was in the middle of the activities. While staying with her daughter at Christmas time she borrowed her daughter's snow suit and goggles, rented a pair of skis and took skiing lessons. "So what's so unusual about that?", you ask; "That is what people do when they visit Colorado." Maybe so, but Ellen had never been on skis before and she was 75 years young already!

Ellen was a risk taker. Knowing that, her son surprised her for her 80th birthday with a hot-air balloon ride. She did admit to having butterflies before the trip, and maybe on her first ascent, but she could not stop chattering about the sights and lack of sounds she experienced in the gondola.

A fellow senior at the center liked to make a play on Ellen's name saying, "no matter how long Ellen lives, she will always be Young!" I wonder if marrying into her husband's Young family was a self-fulfilling prophesy.

ELLEN'S CHARISM

The bequest Ellen left me with has less to do with her name than her spirit and spunk. Ellen met each day as a new and blank page in her life. She taught me not to let age have any affect on being open to a new odyssey. Though I don't think I will be taking skiing lessons at 75, I might try scuba diving lessons. I won't bungee jump but might fly on a zip-line. I resolve to face adventure with the heart of the Young. May I always be willing to seize the opportunity to imitate Ellen's example of boldness in the eye of risk *(though I will probably insist on a safety net)*.

"The tree grew great and strong, its top reached to heaven, and it was visible to the ends of the whole earth. Its foliage was beautiful, its fruit abundant, and it provided food for all. The animals of the field found shade under it, the birds of the air nested in its branches, and from it all living beings were fed."
Daniel 4:11-12

LONG TERM CARE

In the 1960's I served as a Red Cross teen volunteer in our county-managed nursing home. In those days, medical care for the aged and infirm often provided barracks type of housing. There was little, if any privacy. Patients were allotted a small dresser for personal belongings and a single, uncomfortable kitchen type chair for the occasional visitor. I remember writing letters for a woman bed-bound by Multiple Sclerosis. She was mentally alert and well spoken. I sometimes had trouble keeping up with her dictation. I spent the summer helping in that home and never once saw her out of her bed.

Unfortunately, that image of long term care is etched in our minds still today. For most of us, this is a dreaded, feared, even despised stage of aging. We don't want to place our loved ones in a home and we certainly don't want to go there ourselves. However, there often comes a time in caring for our elderly family members that it becomes necessary for placement in a long term care facility – now, however, they are often called a 'rehab center' to avoid the stigma of the term 'nursing home'.

As you might expect, new residents often come from unsafe living conditions. They are frequently isolated by disabilities such as bad eyesight, severe hearing loss, and absentee family members. When brought to a nursing home they are often weak, non-communicative, and ready to die. Some cry for the first few days of residency. After a few more days of adjustment, socialization, routine, meds and meals served on time, they actually show signs of improvement! Some actually become the 'life of the party'!

Today, long term care facilities are governed by stringent state and federal regulations. The décor, lighting and indoor climate control make living conditions are usually quite comfortable – often better than the in-home experience. The food is frequently served family style and often caters to personal preferences. Many homes allow residents to bring furniture, pictures, bedding, and other personal belongings too sentimental to leave behind. The staff are screened, trained and continually educated in caring techniques.

Family, friends and community volunteers are encouraged to make frequent visits. Residents are invigorated by active recreation which often includes physical and mental stimulation. Placement in a nursing home is not the curse it once was. Long term care facilities may not the ideal place to age but as you get to know the folks who live there, you will enjoy the stories of the following characters.

THE SPIRIT INTENDED CONTINUES

Psalm 90 closes with the psalmist crying out to God for mercy. Interestingly, he asks for God's favor to be bestowed on his people as well as himself. Compassion and selflessness is a common, and perhaps the most important legacy passed on to me by my senior mentors.

13 "Turn, O Lord! How long?
　　Have compassion on your servants!
14 Satisfy us in the morning with your steadfast love,
　　so that we may rejoice and be glad all our
　　days.
15 Make us glad as many days as you have afflicted
　　us, and for as many years as we have seen
　　evil.
16 Let your work be manifest to your servants,
　　and your glorious power to their children
17 Let the favor of the Lord our God be upon us,
　　and prosper for us the work of our hands!
　　O prosper the work of our hands!"

(verses 13-17 NRSV)

LURA

"Cherish all your happy moments; they make a fine cushion for old age."

Booth Tarkington

Lura was an unassuming resident in the long term care home she was thin, but not skinny. She was medium height, about 5˙5". She wore slacks and long sleeved flowered print polyester blouses. She wore a lightweight cardigan sweater neatly slung over her narrow shoulders. Her oxford shoes seemed more comfortable to her than slippers. Lura stood as erect as possible while using her walker to stride from her room to the common areas of the home. Her wavy hair, like all the other residents, was a mixture of white and gray, was short and neat. It was her face that set off her entire image: Lura glowed. He skin was soft and appeared younger than her 90+ years, few wrinkles marked the time. Her bright blue eyes were clear and showed no sign of sadness of regret. Her smile was demure giving only a glimpse of her perfect dentures. Lura was not a socialite in the home she was quite comfortable in her room with her books and television.

What drew me to her were her stories. Lura had traveled in her younger years and shared her memories with me many times. One experience I remember her relating happened on a trip to Hawaii. I must admit this story sticks with me today because I heard it several times! But each time she told it I listened as if it was the first time I heard it.

The episode went like this:

"We were on a bus tour of the island. The bus driver seemed to never tire of talking about the points of interest. He kept us all interested with his enthusiasm. A pineapple plantation was our next stop. The driver suggested we all watch out the front window as he maneuvered the bus up a hill and around a curve. There in front of us was an expansive field of pineapples. It was breathtaking. The irrigation system spraying water across the fields made conditions ripe for a beautiful rainbow arching low over the field and the ends reaching to the edges of the field."

I think that was Lura's favorite travel memory. She described it exactly the same each time she shared it. Some would have tired of hearing it but I loved to watch her face as she told it. I know she relived the experience in her mind's eye every time she related the story. I could imagine myself sitting next to her on the bus and witnessing the surprise rainbow as we rounded the curve and topped the hill. I don't need to go to Hawaii because I saw that plantation through Lura's eyes and words.

LURA'S CHARISM

Lura shared more than her travelogues with me. She taught me to be observant. Memories are made in the details of experiences whether those experiences are humdrum or historic, simple or spectacular. I now make it a point to be diligent in observing my surroundings. When I remember an event or place in my life I conjure up a whole picture as Lura did. Just as Lura's memories kept Lura's morale up in what could be depressing life circumstances I too have emblazoned memories of people, places and experiences on my own mind and heart. This practice is even better than scrapbooking because memories are free! Thanks, Lura!

"I remember the days of old, I think about all your deeds, I meditate on the works of your hands."

Psalms 143:5

MARTHA

"The young who has not wept is a savage, the old (wo)man who will not laugh is a fool."

George Santayana

Oh how I dreaded to step into Martha's room. She was such a curmudgeon. She was in the nursing home to rehabilitate from a broken hip. However, she was an unwilling participant in the physical therapy process so she wasn't progressing as fast as the staff would like.

Martha was a long-term divorcee. It must have been a miserable marriage because she had a miserable countenance! The couple had no children. I don't know if that contributed to her misery or if that was a benefit to future generations! Martha complained about anything and everything - incessantly. The room was too cold; the sun was too bright; the food was cold; the food was too hot; the iced tea was weak; the coffee was too strong – and on, and on, and on. Her complaints alienated everyone – staff, fellow residents, visitors, volunteers. An hour with Martha was like a day without sunshine!

As the activity director at that nursing home, it was my job to engage all the residents in some kind of meaningful activity every day. For the bed bound that might include reading from the Bible or bringing recorded classical music to their room. For the active it might include an exercise class. For Martha it meant listening to her complaining conversation.

Weekends in that nursing home were usually bustling with family visitors. No one ever came to visit Martha. She had a kind hearted neighbor at home who was caring for Martha's two cats, but that person did not make visitation a priority. She obviously liked the cats better than Martha!

One late winter Saturday, I had arranged for teens from the Future Farmers of America to bring some baby farm animals to the nursing home. Many of our residents had lived on farms before entering residency so I knew this activity would bring out a crowd. The teens brought rabbits, chickens, kittens, sheep, and even a calf. Because it was still chilly outdoors, all of the animals were brought indoors – yes, even the calf.

The residents loved the show! There was a hum of chatter that drew people from their rooms to the large crowd congregating in the large day room. The staff brought those who could not propel their own wheelchairs. It was great fun!

The best part of the animals' visitation was the miracle we all witnessed that day. One of the teens placed a large docile rabbit in Martha's lap. The rabbit sat in her lap for close to an hour, allowing Martha to pet him the whole time. Her hard heart melted in front of our eyes. As she stroked the soft brown creature in her lap, Martha actually smiled! She began to tell of former pets and the cats being cared for at home. She was actually pleasant! When it was time for the teens to take the animals back to their respective farms Martha was the last to give up her 'pet for a day'.

MARTHA'S CHARISM

To witness a curmudgeon's metamorphosis into a marshmallow is an event I will never forget. Martha's legacy is the understanding that even the coldest heart can be warmed by the unconditional love of an animal. To really appreciate Martha's charism, I must give some credit to the rabbit. The effect the rabbit had on her did not last much beyond his visit that day but I arranged for animal visits often after that day and Martha was always included on 'the guest list'!

"For everything there is a season, a time for every matter under the heaven…a time to love, and a time to hate…"

Ecclesiastes 5:1,8

CLYDE

"I think you're old at about 70. That's when you have to make a grunting noise every time you get up from a chair."

Clyde came to the central Arkansas on a covered wagon when he was 21 years old. He and his brother drove a team of horses, tethering an extra horse and an ox across the swamplands of the Mississippi delta. The brothers crossed streams on foot to guide the team safely and crossed the 'Mighty Mississip' on a ferry. They averaged about 10 miles a day. They slept under the stars at night. They spent two weeks on the trail before reaching their destination. He told me the story several times. I became as proud of it as he was and often shared it myself.

Clyde lived in 'my' nursing home for the last five years of his life. For most, that time would have been unhappy and full of pain, loss, and loneliness. Not so for Clyde. He was a man, who made the best of less than an ideal situation. Clyde was remarkable. He was always patient and kind to those around him. Everyone loved him – staff and fellow residents alike.

Clyde was over ninety when I met him. He was hard of hearing – deaf as the proverbial door nail! You could hear his TV blaring from down the hall. His eyes were good – beyond your wildest imagination. The daily paper was delivered to his private room and he could read it without the aid of glasses! His mind was like that of a man a third his age. He comprehended the news and shared his opinion of current events, but only when asked. Clyde was a gentleman, humble and unassuming.

Clyde would often entertain his friends with his piano playing. He played many songs from memory but could also read from the home's library of sheet music. Having grown up involved in church, his favorite tunes included a repertoire of Gospel Music. After all, God was his personal friend.

Living in a nursing home can be taxing and depressing for those who are mentally fit but Clyde never let that bother him. Like most long term care facilities, Clyde's home hosted some wanderers. Folks walked aimlessly in and out of rooms, up and down the halls. It seemed their favorite rooms were those other than their own. Often the wanderers would pick up something laying on a neighbor's chair or a bed and deposit it in the next room. Other alert residents like Clyde had little patience with these 'movers and takers'. Clyde did, he never spoke a harsh word to any wanderer. He had a remarkable compassion for those less fortunate than himself.

While living at the nursing home, Clyde met a lady resident, Leah, who matched both his cognitive and his physical abilities. They were nearly inseparable, eating together and visiting for hours in the day room. Although I seldom knew what was so funny, they laughed together often.

Clyde loved to recount this story:

"You know, Leah is heels over head in love with me. I know that because she came to visit me in my room. She looked around for a place to sit and decided to join me in my laid back recliner." I failed to describe Leah's ample size. "I wasn't expecting her to plop down so hard. We fell over backward and there we were – heels over heads!" He went on, still laughing as he continued his story, "We were laughing so loud and hard that the nurses at the station heard us and came running. They found our four feet kicking in the air and thought we were crying in pain! Once they knew we were okay, they laughed too. It took two nurses and the maintenance man to get Leah and me up!" After these antics, the couple was sternly admonished not to share the chair again!

Clyde and Leah where quite 'an item'; they even discussed getting married but decided against it. Their bond continued and Clyde was there to comfort Leah as she was dying of Cancer. He wept when she finally passed away. Then he went on with his life – watching the TV, reading the newspaper, visiting other residents, being a gentleman. He knew God and knew his own death was not far off. Past ninety he had a lot of practice at not looking back.

It seemed that Clyde lived to be patient and kind to those around him. He epitomized the meaning of the word 'gentleman'. May I emulate Clyde's life and be proud of my humble beginnings, enjoy the middle of my life, and don't be afraid of the end. May we all die as Clyde did: peacefully, with a smile on his face.

"...you shall take the fruit of majestic trees, branches of palm trees, boughs of leafy trees, and willows of the brook; and you shall rejoice before the Lord your God for seven days."

Leviticus 23:40

HENRY AND DOVIE

"My eyes have seen much, but they are not weary.
My ears have heard much, but they thirst for more."

Rabindranath Tagore

I didn't meet Henry and Dovie until they were forced by failing health, to leave their home and enter the nursing home. On the surface, their story was remarkable based on their long marriage. They were married 77 years! I had the privilege of interviewing the couple and writing a newspaper article about them. Being married that long was certainly newsworthy. Even the nationally televised weatherman, Willard Scott, was impressed.

We spent hours together as I questioned the couple about their life together. They shared many stories. They met at a community barn dance. Henry courted her driving his father's horse and buggy to her family's farm. When they spoke of marriage, Dovie told me that her mother wanted them to get married by a preacher. They were frugal even in their youth. Dovie didn't want any of the fuss of a big wedding; Henry didn't want to spend a lot of money. Both insisted that they would elope. Henry picked Dovie up in a borrowed wagon pulled by a big roan horse.

After they married, the couple 'took up farming'. Working together they built a modest house on their land. They told of plowing fields with mules. When Henry told of losing babies Dovie hushed him. She told him matter of factly, "change the subject". He did, without question, and never mentioned them again.

When the dust bowl of the 30's forced them from the farm, they went where they could find work and 'bloomed where they were planted'. In Kansas City Henry did some roofing until he fell off a ladder. After he healed they headed back to the familiarity of farm life and eked out a living there.

They worked together to raise two sons and a daughter to adulthood. They were proud that none of them ever got in trouble with the law.

Throughout the interview I was impressed by how sharp Henry's and Dovie's minds were at their advanced ages. Henry was 97 and Dovie was 95! Henry was blind and Dovie was hearing impaired. Even in the frailty of their old age, together they made a good team! They certainly had not set out to live so long but they *did* set out to be married until 'death do you part.'

At home, while I was writing the tribute article, I wondered how Henry and Dovie had lived so long. In proofing the article before sending it to the newspaper I discovered what I believe is the reason for their longevity. Throughout the article, as each told their respective story, I had described their demeanor. The binding thread throughout was humor. Yes, a simple chuckle, a belly laugh, a smile or a snicker, showed up again and again.

THEIR CHARISM

'Experts on aging' tell us aging well requires constant learning. Those who live long lives often credit their longevity to hard work and clean living. 'Experts' tell us how to lead our lives. Eat this; don't eat that. Start an exercise program today; get a doctor's okay before starting to exercise. The contradictory list goes on and on. I worked with the elderly over 20 years and I think that makes *me* an 'expert' of sorts. This expert has decided that the key to Henry's and Dovie's long life together is laughter. They have put the bad things behind them and didn't allow each other to bring it up. They made light of the tribulations that came along in life and laughed easily at mistakes they made.

What is Henry's and Dovie's charism? To laugh well is to live well. To laugh long is to live long. Change the subject when necessary. Love to laugh and laugh to love. View yourself and those around you with humor. Learn to laugh at yourself; but be careful to laugh only *with* someone else.

"Wives, be subject to your husbands as you are to the Lord...Husbands, love your wives, just as Christ loved the church and gave himself up for her..."
Ephesians 5:22, 25

CLARA

*"Outwardly I am 83, but inwardly I am every age, with the
emotions and experiences of each period."*

Elizabeth Coatsworth

Clara considered herself a socialite in her time. She
graduated from the State Teachers' College at a time when women
attended college to snatch up a man destined to make a mark in the
world. Women, after all, were expected to marry and stay home and
raise children. Clara fulfilled all those goals – she snagged a
successful man, married, and stayed home to raise their two
daughters. Clara's husband grew into an administrative position with
the same college from which she graduated. Clara grew into the role
of the supportive wife. They hosted staff and community parties.
Everyone in the community wanted to be invited to her soirees.
Clara served on the boards of directors for several non-profit
agencies on and off campus, often being the first to volunteer to
chair a committee.

Sadly, a dark cloud hung over Clara's home. In the 'old days'
Clara would have been classified as manic depressive; today the
disease is known as bi-polar. Whatever you call it Clara's life, and
the lives of her family was topsy-turvy. When she was 'up', in the
manic stage, she had the energy of the Energizer Bunny and
everybody loved being around her. She was the life of the party and
served as chief fund raiser for many a gala. When she was down, she
was self indulgent, demanding, and irascible. Nothing and no one
could please her. This depressive stage was often bad enough to
require hospitalization.

The constant barometric pressure swing in the household
affected the children. They would dutifully appear at parties to be
shown off, like prized possessions during parties served during
Clara's 'up' stage. They would hide in the closets or under the beds
during the 'down' stage.

As she aged, arthritis took a toll on Clara's skeleton. Being
the difficult personality that she was, her daughters had no recourse

but to seek nursing home placement; her husband had died a few years earlier. She was in a wheel chair when I met her. She was young for nursing home placement. Interestingly, her father was still alive and lived in his own home. He had a caregiver whom Clara despised. Clara suspected the caregiver was taking advantage of her father.

Clara was fairly independent, needing little help from the staff for what is called, activities of daily living (dressing, toileting, personal care, etc.). Her daughters took good care of Clara's financial affairs. She was free to order gifts for her friends from local boutiques and have them delivered. She had a standing appointment to have her hair done in the facility's beauty shop. The daily newspaper was delivered to her and she devoured the community news. She had more magazines delivered to her than all of the other residents combined! She attended every activity offered by the activity director. Faithful friends visited often. It could have been an ideal residency, except her family was fractured. Neither her daughters, nor her grown grandchildren, nor her father visited.

CLARA'S CHARISM

Clara and I bonded. I didn't know her history. From my observation point, I didn't understand the dynamics and thought her family was remiss. Over time I was enlightened by other staff, Clara's old friends, and her daughters. While Clara and I maintained a mutual respect I softened toward her family. Clara's scenario helped me grow in wisdom. What I learned has served me well.

The lesson in Clara's spirit is the insight to accept reality - that time does not heal all wounds. Sometimes we can't make amends and must endure the consequences of our behaviors. We have a responsibility to others to apologize, ask for, and then pray for, forgiveness. We must also forgive others.

One more piece to Clara's legacy is that forgiveness does not always produce a close relationship. The hurt is often deeper that the soul can reconcile.

Clara took to her bed one day in a depressive state and turned off her will to live. I had often heard of people willing themselves to die but Clara was the first person I witnessed doing that. God rest her soul, I'm sure she is finally at peace. I hope her family is too.

"By the streams the birds of the air have their habitation; they sing among the branches. From your lofty abode you water the mountains; the earth is satisfied with the fruit of your work."

Psalm 104:12-13

EDNA

"Grey hair is God's graffiti."

Bill Cosby

Alzheimer's disease robs a family of their loved one twice; once in the dementia of life and again in the finality of death. Along the journey families are encouraged to laugh and make time to heal. I observed one such healing while working on a secured dementia unit in a nursing home.

Edna came to us from another facility because she was what is called 'an elopement risk'. She was a regular Houdini – an escape artist. That facility was on a major highway and her family realized the hazard in her behavior. To make the situation more dangerous, she recruited other residents to elope with her!

The safety of our specialized secure unit drew the family to place Edna with us despite the 50 mile distance from her home town. She flourished in her new surroundings. She thought she was living in a hotel. This impression was conceivable by the small private dining room, the bright cozy sitting room, fenced patio, non-institutional room décor, and most importantly, the lack of an overhead speaker system.

Edna's daughter, Linda, worked full time but had Wednesdays off. Each week Linda would come and use the facility's beauty shop to wash, set and style Edna's snow white hair. Edna reveled in the attention. The primping provided time for seemingly senseless girl talk.

EDNA'S CHARISM

There was a silver lining to the effects of Alzheimer's disease. Linda shared her family history with me. Apparently Linda's birth had been difficult and Edna never fully recovered from post-partum depression. She was verbally abusive to Linda in her childhood and overbearing during Linda's teen years. Linda yearned to experience a mother's unconditional love. This sad history was never evident in Linda's care for Edna. They spent several happy hours together each week.

What Alzheimer's stole from Edna was a memory of anger and resentment. What Alzheimer's gave to Linda was healing. That was a beautiful legacy for both Linda and me!

I thank them both that I had the opportunity to witness the restoration of a broken family. Their mended relationship taught me that mercy has no timeline; it is possible that something good can come out of a tragic diagnosis.

"A shoot shall come out from the stock of Jesse, and a branch shall grow out of his roots. The spirit of the Lord shall rest on him, the spirit of wisdom and understanding the spirit of counsel and, the spirit of knowledge and the fear of the Lord."

Psalm 11:1-2

SHORT BUT POWERFUL ANECDOTES

There are people who enter our lives and stay for just a little while but make a big impact. These are some of those people who have left an indelible mark on my character in the short time I knew them.

LUNA

"Old people who shine from the inside look 10 to 20 years younger."

Dolly Parton

Being on a limited income never bothered Luna. She was in touch with God on a daily basis and wanted for little. While she walked to and from the Senior Dining Site, Luna enjoyed the beauty of God's nature. While she baked her famous apple pie, she thanked God for the gift of a bountiful harvest. While she carried that pie to a neighbor's house, she prayed that the pie would bring enjoyment to those who ate it. You could actually *hear* the peace-filled smile on her face when you talked to her on the phone.

Luna walked to lunch early one morning just to share her 'good news'. She told us this little story. "I got up this morning and enjoyed my new carpet." Someone asked her with a voice laced with envy, "How can you afford new carpet?" Luna smiled knowingly. "When I went to bed last night my front yard was grassy green. This morning there was a four inch layer of golden leaves all over the yard!" Most people would have cursed nature's leaf drop knowing that it meant hours of back breaking raking. Not Luna, she admired "God's gift of 'new carpet'!"

Luna left me a wonderful bequest, one that I enjoy on a daily, sometimes an hourly basis! She taught me to pay attention to my surroundings; to look for God's hand in any and all phenomenon; and to thank him for it all! Thanks, Luna, you were a precious gift to me. I thank God for the opportunity to know you!

HAROLD

"We get too soon old, and too late smart."

German proverb

Although Harold was a painter by trade but he could carve wood, fix appliances, change the oil in his truck – blindfolded! He was a bona-fide jack-of-all-trades. His hero must have been the inventor, Leonardo da'Vinci!

Harold was a generous man. He gave us gallons of paint for our home rehab project. He gave his neighbors a ride to the local Senior Dining Site regularly. Once there, he volunteered, helping the staff serve his fellow seniors. He told corny jokes, always trying to put a smile on a curmudgeon's face.

HAROLD'S CHARISM

Harold's legacy is not a character builder or a legacy of values; yet what Harold taught me makes my life easier on a daily basis. He watched me tie and re-tie my shoes several times a day. One day he stopped me, told me to sit down, and said "I'm going to teach you to tie your shoes!"

This will make more sense if you sit down and hold one tail of your shoe laces in each hand. Throw the right lace over and under the left lace; before pulling the lace ends tight, repeat this step; then pull the lace ends tight. This makes the foundation knot 'loose proof!' Now, complete the motion you use to make a bow and pull it tight. It sounds so simple but the laces stay tied tight all day!

At Harold's urging, I tried this on curling ribbon, leather laces, satin ribbon, yarn, and rope. With this knot technique, there is no need to bring in a volunteer finger placement on the initial knot to hold it from slipping when you are wrapping Christmas presents. I'm telling you, I have never had this fail!

We left from that house for which Harold furnished paint but I have never left untied shoe laces trip me up! Thanks, Harold, what a genius idea!

KAY

"It's funny how you can go through life thinking you've seen everything...then suddenly realize there are millions of things you've never seen before."

Charles Shulz

Kay was a young looking 75 year old when I met her. She lived in senior housing, but seldom socialized with her fellow residents. She was a published author, and still enjoyed journaling. Kay spent her time knitting, and reading, and watching VHS movies. Though she walked with a cane, Kay still drove and could go where she wanted, when she wanted. She told me she was her own best friend. Kay did not feel the need for companionship.

My job at the time that I met her was to survey the little community in which she lived for the possibility of opening a senior meal site. Kay was supportive though she wasn't interested in attending. Her independent spirit included cooking talents.

State funding for the meal site was approved and I was there for the grand opening. Kay was too! At first she came one day a week; then two; then three; eventually, daily! Her gait improved and she used her cane less and less. She confessed to me that, "I didn't know how lonely I was until I started coming here."

As Kay grew more sociable, she 'took up company' with one of the gentlemen who also frequented the meal site. They became quite an item. Naturally, there was gossip but it bothered neither of them. They planned on marrying! Alas, the man died before the nuptials. Kay took the loss well but was pleased when the man's family gave her his cane as a memento.

KAY'S CHARISM

Kay gave me some very important lessons. She taught me to disregard what others think. I will not waste time lamenting what might have been, nor will I worry about what might be. Kay stayed busy, reading, writing, building friendships. I want to be like Kay – be my own best friend while developing more best friends!

TOM *AND HIS CHARISM*

"Every man's memory is his private literature!"
Aldous Huxley

Tom was a retired military veteran. I didn't know him very well but I expect he was an officer in the army! He had one speed – fast. To describe Tom as a take-charge, bull headed guy is an understatement. He spearheaded a tomato harvest for the senior center's summertime fundraiser Taco Salad Luncheon.

Tom insisted a crew of staff and senior volunteers drive out to the farm fields to pick bushels of tomatoes for the taco salads. We knew better than to protest. By the next morning, each one of our four person crew carried a large box into very muddy acreage. Migrant workers were just across the dirt farm road picking the firm baseball sized red tomatoes for a local cannery. Fearing repercussions, I dared to ask Tom if we had the grower's permission to pick in that quadrant. His answer? "It is easier to ask forgiveness than permission!"

The morning went smoothly, except the mud was up to our knees and it was difficult to move among the rows. Before the sun was overhead we had enough tomatoes to serve a taco salad to every man, woman and child in the county!

By the way, we did not have to ask forgiveness because Tom had indeed discussed our hunt for red tomatoes with the owner. Though he was pulling my leg, I did not forget his life lesson of, "it is easier to ask forgiveness than permission!"

"Finally, all of you, have unity of spirit, sympathy, love for one another, a tender heart, and a humble mind. Do not repay evil for evil or abuse for abuse; but on the contrary, repay with a blessing."

1 Peter: 8-9

A Seed Was Planted and
Spirituality Began To Grow

THE ROOTS OF MY AWARENESS

GRANDMA

"Old age is for the birds!"

Frieda Geary,
better known to me as Grandma

It is important to remember that age was perceived differently in 'the old days'. Men worked outside the home. The women worked inside the home: keeping the home fires burning by cooking, cleaning, washing, ironing, taking care of the children, community volunteering, and on and on. At retirement, the man sat down. If he was out of the house it was to golf or bowl. The woman did not have an opportunity to retire; she carried on her busy nurturing routine.

To describe Grandma as old is an understatement; she was born in 1894 for goodness sake. Her hair was silvery-gray and worn in a bun. Her face and hands were wrinkled. She needed glasses to read the newspaper and to knit but not to drive. She was petite and to make up for her height she wore black oxfords with two inch heels - "nun shoes", like the women in habits used to wear. Around the house, Grandma wore 'dusters' decorated with tiny flowers and that closed with 'snappers' rather than buttons. Out in public Grandma wore simple gingham dresses. In my youthful memory, Grandma was the classic 'little old lady'.

I did the math recently, calculating her birth year, my birth year, and my age at my earliest recollections of Grandma. The sum total? The grandmother in my early memories must have been a mere 62. Today, 62 is almost 'middle age'!

Grandma lived in a traditional bungalow with dark brown shingle siding. A green porch swing hung at one end of the front-porch. She lived in small town America; a friendly, safe place, with sidewalks, streetlights, and neighborhood storefronts. I am almost certain that every phone in that small town was black with no dial. Calls were directed by a human telephone company employee who asked "Num-ber, Pl-e-a-se?" when you picked up the heavy receiver. Telephone operators stretched out their words in those days, pronouncing each letter individually. It was a town where neighbors actually used the sidewalks to visit neighbors, walk to church, and Trick-Or-Treat.

Grandma's lifestyle was iconic. She was a housewife. She was happy in that role. She was a great cook. Sunday dinners were shared with family at her house. When she made sauerkraut it smelled up the whole neighborhood! I'm sure it smelled good to some but personally, I could not get past the odor so I never even tasted it!

She watched us kids after school, often keeping us overnight while my mother helped my father start a business. Grandma could multi-task before the word was even invented! She knitted with one eye on the sweater in progress and one eye on us kids. Grandma always had patience with us. I remember her rocking my young brother for hours trying to quiet his incessant crying during frequent ear-aches.

There was a time that I left my favorite doll on her back door stoop, causing her to fall down the stairs. She broke two ribs in that fall and never told my mother how she fell – she didn't want to get me into trouble! We respected her authority and she never had to raise her voice to keep us under control because she could send chills down our spines by giving us her 'grandma eyes'.

Grandma took her wedding vows seriously; 'for better or for worse, in sickness and in health, 'til death us do part.' Hers and Grandpa's marriage withstood more than most. Their house burned to the ground in the middle of a harsh winter when my uncles were toddlers. They lost everything except a perambulator. While the fire was still burning someone stole that baby carriage out of the front yard. There were looters even in 1918!.

Sometime after the fire, Grandpa was on 'daddy duty' and the baby, Billy, fell down the basement steps at 18 months old. He survived the fall but died shortly afterward of meningitis. Grandma told me the story when my own child was about 18 months old. She blamed the death on the fall. That might explain why the one photo of my grandparents standing apart from each other is at the cemetery. I learned that sadness of such a loss never goes away. Statistically the loss of a child breaks marriages more often than not. That was certainly 'for worse' but Grandma took her wedding vows seriously.

She grieved when her father was killed in a car accident. He and her mother lived in a small town with narrow country roads, and cars were not as safe as they are today. Small town medicine couldn't save him. A few years later, Grandma was called away from her mothering duties and she temporarily moved to the same small country town in which her father was killed. Her mother was dying and it was Grandma's turn to take care of her. My mother was about eight years old and missed her terribly.

My uncle joined the Navy and sailed away to see the world. On a short home-visit he brought a young sailor from California home. He and my mother fell in love and corresponded for some time. We had just entered the war and my father was on his way to the South Pacific. The wedding was to be in California, too far away for Grandma to make the trip– money was tight and gas rationing was in full swing. That was a lifelong disappointment for Grandma.

My grandfather worked until the day he was paralyzed by a stroke at 74 years old. Grandma took care of him herself until he died at 85. Those last 11 years of Grandpa's life were not idle for either of them. They moved from New York to Florida – it took three moves to finally settle in to a 'permanent' address. Despite my grandfather's paralysis, Grandma drove them to California. That was a five day drive before the Inter-state system was complete across the country. Grandma bragged that she never drove after dark either way!

As time passed, the most amazing thing happened; Grandma experienced a metamorphosis. She no longer wore those ugly 'nun shoes' opting for white sling back sandals – comfortable but classy. Her wardrobe blossomed with bright colored flowers, dusters were exchanged for pantsuits. She had her soft grey hair cut and curled in an easy-to-care-for style. It seemed that as I aged, Grandma got younger!

Grandma was a great story teller. One of my favorite family stories is this:

My great-grandparents were saloon keepers in New York City. At street level was a restaurant and bar; the basement held a bowling alley; upstairs there were two apartments. As newly-weds, my grandparents lived in one and my great-grandparents lived in the other. The business was begun before Prohibition. After Prohibition was passed they continued to operate the saloon 'under the table'.

Grandpa was a New York City fireman. Thinking that he would not be suspected of bootlegging, he would travel to New Jersey - across state lines - and pick up homemade bathtub gin – in his uniform! Back in New York, the gin would be colored and hidden in case of a raid. The law allowed the Federal Agents to search the owner's apartment for bootlegged liquor. Grandpa risked his career for is in-laws and Grandma did her share by secreting the contraband in her apartment.

The best part of the story is this:

Grandma put the containers of gin under a barrel. She covered the barrel with a pretty blue tablecloth. On top she placed two candles…and a statue of the Blessed Mother!

The theory was: Mary asked Jesus to change the water into wine at the marriage feast at Cana. Grandma asked Mary to guard the gin from the 'feds'!

Grandma was impish. It was her turn to bring homemade cookies and the recipe to her weekly knitting group. She didn't have time to bake that day. She was busy running after us kids all day. What did she do? She emptied a package of store bought animal cookies into a candy tin to present the cookies as homemade. She didn't stop there. She sat down and made up a recipe – I suspect it was a tongue in cheek literary masterpiece – and took it all to the knitting group meeting!

Grandma was full of wise sayings: "take your coat off or it won't do you any good when you go outside; play like nice little sisters; old age is for the birds." The adage she gave me and I pass on to others on a regular basis is this: "you do what you have to do when you have to do it; there will be time later to wonder how you did it." I have pulled on that wisdom and inner strength each time I've faced a distasteful task. Following her advice made my adjustment easier when career changes forced my family to leave a home I loved and move across country. As I got out and made new friends in each new hometown, that same wise adage carried me through transition. When I went back to school at 50 years old, I lived by that truism. Grandma was right, I did what I had to do … and I still wonder how I did it!

Grandma was an exceptional lady. She was more than happy, she was content. Grandma is gone now. She lived to be 92 years young. Her great grandchildren got to know her and she left them with some of the same grandma-isms she left me. The ripple continues, but I often offer this prayer, "You have made my life richer. You helped me find a career I loved; one in which I learned a lot and grew into the person I am today. Thanks, Grandma."

GRANDMA'S CHARISM

Grandma left me many spiritual legacies: love, strength, sense of family, but I think the best, and most important, was respect for the aged. Grandma planted an acorn in my garden. I tended it, fertilized it, and let it grow into a giant oak tree of service. Because of my love for Grandma I was drawn to an Area Agency on Aging to apply for my first adult job. That part-time job led to a twenty year career working in congregate meal sites, senior centers, assisted living and long term care facilities. Through my life's work I've known so many characters – some productive and others useless, many strong but some weak, some miserable but most lighthearted. I learned something from every one of them. And I have never lost my passion for the elderly. There is a bonus to Grandma's legacy - I don't fear aging as so many of my peers do, in fact, I embrace aging – many are denied the privilege.

I maintain that there is freedom in aging!

"Grandchildren are the crown of the aged, and the glory of children is their (grand)parents."

Psalm 17:6

THE LAST WORDS

Someone asked me, "What is the most important lesson you learned from your senior mentors?" That is the *Million Dollar Question*. However I have pondered another, more personal and pertinent question, "Which spiritual value lessons, which charisms, do I hope to pass on to my family?" It would be easy to answer that if cloning my personal values developed by years of experience was a possibility.

Let's look to literature for the answer.

- William Shakespeare wrote a famous eulogy for Julius Caesar given by Brutus, one of Caesar's most trusted friends and also one of his murderers. Brutus called to his "Friends, Romans, countrymen, lend me your ears. I have come to bury Caesar, not to praise him. The evil men do lives after them; the good they do is oft interred with their bones..." I pray that the good I try to practice in my daily life will provide my charism.

- St. Francis of Assisi is quoted as saying, "Preach the gospel always, and if necessary, use words." I pray that I am preaching and passing on the teachings of the gospel by my daily life example – and that will provide my charism.

- The American Poet Laureate, Robert Frost, wrote a poem entitled...

The Road Not Taken

Two roads diverged in a yellow wood,
And sorry I could not travel both
And be one traveler, long I stood
And I looked down one as far as I could
To where it bent in the undergrowth;
Then took the other, as just as fair,
And having perhaps the better claim,
Because it was grassy and wanted wear;
Though as for that the passing there
Had worn them really about the same,
And both that morning equally lay
In leaves no step had trodden black.
Oh, I kept the first for another day!
Yet knowing how way leads on to way,
I doubted if I should ever come back.
I shall be telling this with a sigh
Somewhere ages and ages hence:
Two roads diverged in a wood, and I –
I took the one less travelled by,
And that has made all the difference.

I have spent many years working with and for the elderly – taking care of their physical, social, emotional, and familial well beings. This is not a career for the faint of heart. It hurts when they hurt. It hurts when their family members share an ugly transgression. It hurts when they die. The triumph comes in the spiritual legacy each leaves behind.

One piece of advice I offer to those living with, dealing with, working with, and visiting with the elderly is to listen to the repetitive stories each time as if it were the first! It is in listening to those stories that we help others to develop their legacy, their **Seasoned Spirituality**. Aging should be embraced – like tree hugging! There is a great freedom to be found in aging – for one thing, we can be very blunt, we are allowed to forget the painful, and we have the right to be wrong!

We go through life influencing others barely aware that anyone is watching. If I can be an enviable example for someone and that example lives on after me, then I have succeeded in recycling a CHARISM left to me by my mentors that others will want to emulate.

Now is the time for us to pass on our own spiritual legacies to future generations. Let those charisms reflect those which others passed on to us! Each day we have the opportunity to tend the garden of life. We plant seeds, fertilize soil, pull weeds, eliminate invasive pests, and enjoy the harvest. Along the way we must remember that it all takes work – planting can be back breaking, fertilizing makes our hands dirty and smelly, weeding brings blisters, eliminating pests often brings bites and stings. The harvest finally comes; we reap the benefits of all that struggle and work and are happy to share the abundance. Wisdom is like the harvest – wisdom must be shared, for it is in passing along life's values that ensures that we can continue to inhabit God's creation.

Enter the garden; begin the hard work of gardening. Remember that life takes hard work. Love takes hard work. Peace takes hard work. It all starts with a seed. Plant an acorn and grow a mighty oak – plant a life value and improve society.

"We need old friends to help us grow old and new friends to help us stay young!"

Letty Cottin Pogrebin

THE VALUE OF TREES

"Wrinkles should merely indicate where smiles have been."
Mark Twain

Trees shelter us, trees feed us, trees heal us. The value of the tree is in its inherent quality for good. Many stories have been written about life lessons learned by observing trees. The children's book, The Giving Tree, is a fine example; the Legend of The Three Trees is another. Look for these and share the timeless stories with the young people in your life.

The wood harvested from a tree is part of our everyday lives. Consider the lowly pencil. It is an unassuming tool which can change lives by the words produced by its use. It can enhance the quality of life by the art work produced by its exercise. Trees and their roots have contributed to health and healing in many cultures. The history of civilization can be told in examining fine furniture. Furniture from past centuries and monarchies is displayed in museums around the world: Louis XVI, Queen Anne, Napoleon, and Victoria. American furniture also contributes to the chronicling of history through: the simplicity of the American colonial period, the utilitarianism of the Shaker influence, and the sleek lines of mid-century modern. All add beauty to function. Examine the large hand-carved doors serving as entrances to centuries-old European churches. The trees used to make their doors left a legacy for millions of visitors despite being cut down. Art and architecture show off the qualities of wood that we treasure most – the strength, the grain and texture.

So it is with the aged. The most humble, unassuming man can change lives by the words uttered if one will only listen. The gnarled hands can produce a beautiful candlestick or a sturdy walking stick each enhancing life. The personal experiences of the elderly helped make the history of our world. The senior citizen has crossed the threshold of the church doors thousands, no, hundreds of thousands of times. They know God – personally. The elderly are to be treasured for their strength and their flaws, their rough exteriors and wrinkles as well as the youth and beauty that once was. Each senior leaves a legacy in life and death. It is time, now, to review your life and decide on a legacy of your own.

*"If your experiences would benefit anybody,
give them to someone."*

Florence Nightingale

*"For we write to you nothing other than what you can read and also
understand; I hope you will understand until the end…"*

2 Corinthians 1:13-14

About the Author

Jean Riise Leffler's spirituality can be explained by her life experiences. Through observations of her surroundings and the people in them her relationship with God grows daily. She and husband, David, share a long-term mixed faith marriage. They raised two daughters with the benefit of many of the charisms described within these pages. Some of their free time is spent carrying on lessons learned from Lloyd and others, along with their four grandchildren, by portraying living history at community events.

"For those who desire life and desire to see good days, let them keep their tongues from evil and their lips from speaking deceit; let them turn away from evil and do good; let them seek peace and pursue it. For the eyes of the Lord are on the righteous and his ears are open to their prayer. But the face of the Lord is against those who do evil."

1 Peter 3:10-12

WE ARE A SUM TOTAL OF THE GOOD WE FIND IN OUR
EXPERIENCE

Thank you for sharing in my experiences.
May you develop charisms of your own.
God bless you!

Made in the USA
Charleston, SC
06 March 2014